THE SPIRITUAL VALUE
OF GEM STONES

by

Wally and Jenny Richardson

as channeled through

Lenora Huett

DeVorss & Company, Publishers
P.O. Box 550
Marina del Rey, California 90294-0550

Lovingly dedicated
to those who seek
to transcend
the lower planes of
human consciousness

CONTENTS

Foreword

The information within this book on the spiritual value of stones and minerals has all been channeled from "beyond the veil" of human consciousness. No pre-conceived ideas regarding the historical lore of stones were used; no pre-supposed information was presented as "source material" for the book other than that which refers to the historical relationships between the signs of the zodiac, the months of the year and their corresponding "birth stones." All that you will read has been given to mankind by members of The Great White Brotherhood, and one in particular who is identified only as the "Master of the Mind." Through their great love for humanity and their desire that all souls better understand the relationships between the various kingdoms in nature, has this information been given.

To bring this forth requires a spiritual channel, one who can tap the higher planes of consciousness in a clear and concise manner while remaining in the conscious, physical state. Such a channel is Lenora Huett, co-author of "The Path To Illumination" and "The Amnesia Factor."

To properly understand what a true, spiritual channel is, takes a certain amount of knowledge of the esoteric teachings. It should not be confused with psychic phenomena, or that information tapped from the astral plane of consciousness through the solar plexus center of the receiver.

To become a true spiritual channel requires much diligence over many incarnations, and necessitates a factual alignment between the soul and the "High-self," or God-presence of that individual. To start this long process first requires an alignment between the brain and the soul; this alignment process involves all the three aspects of the personality—that is, the etheric body, the astral vehicle and the mind nature, and is generally developed while the soul is evolving on the "probationary path." In later incarnations, when the soul is well on the path of Discipleship, it begins to build the bridge or "antahkarana" between the soul and the High-self. When this bridge has been built, the "channel" learns to bypass the astral vehicle and the soul or causal body. It also requires a conscious cleansing of the sub-conscious mind.

This process of "bypassing" takes much time and must be worked at with intensity, first of all with the focus upon the emotional nature through conscious discrimination, and finally upon the soul nature under the inspiration of the Spiritual Triad which is eventually substituted for the soul. When this has been done, a direct channel is created, allowing impressions directed by a higher source than the personality to descend into the brain.

All this takes many incarnations, for the registration and the interpretation of the higher impressions is a basic esoteric science and takes much concentration and application to perfect. For those not yet acquainted with true spiritual channelling, this method has been one form used down through the aeons, to bring that information necessary for mankind to recall their true nature as spiritual beings, and to help them physically and materially as they struggle on in the lower octaves of light.

The actual physical work in preparing and bringing this material forward required two separate functions. First, questions had to be prepared on the various gems to be considered, so that intelligent questions could be asked through the channel. This necessitated a study of the many groups and classifications of stones and minerals, so that a comprehensive range would be covered, and also to aid the questioner in understanding some of the material that was channelled through that needed to be expanded upon. The questions, the format and the basic responsibility for assembling this information was given to Wally Richardson.

When the time came for a particular channelling session to begin, no mystical incantations were given, no incense burned, nothing of a psychic nature was employed. We would merely sit down at a table where it was quiet and place before us a tape recorder, a series of questions and usually a variety of stones that would be under discussion for that session. A prayer for love and guidance would be given, asking that only that which is for the highest and best good for humanity be given. After a short moment of silence, while Lenora would center down her consciousness and move it to one side, there would flow through her the words, "Master of the mind," and this was our signal to begin the session. This usually was followed by a message of instruction or guidance or a word of encouragement to keynote the period of channelling, after which the questions would begin.

When it was felt that a wide enough variety of stones had been covered and the material transcribed into a cohesive form, we then went over all of the material through the channel to see if that which was presented was accurate or if there was a need or desire for an expansion of any of the information presented to us. In doing this, we realized that in order for the reader to properly understand and use the material presented, he would need to have a basic under-standing of the endocrine glandular system and the chakra centers which overlie and influence these glands. While there are many books available on these subjects, we would highly recommend "The Chakras," by C. W. Leadbeater, Theosophi-cal Pub. House, Wheaton, Ill., and "Glands—Our Invisible Guardians," by M. W. Kapp, M.D., Rosicrucian Press, San Jose, Calif. In addition, there are several good books by A. E.

Powell dealing with the emotional and mental bodies that will add a lot to your comprehension of the material following.

There were many additional stones that could have been covered, much additional information that could have been uncovered, and even some material that could not be divulged, not because of any harm that could ensue, but because of the powerful force of greed that is still predominant and flows unchecked in many souls today.

We have referred to The Great White Brotherhood as the source material for this book, and doubtless there are many who have never heard or been aware of their existence. The White Brotherhood has nothing to do with the color of a man's skin. It refers to those who are considered to be the "Holy Spirits," rather than "Holy Spirit," which so often has been used throughout the literature of the Holy Bible. Many are called Holy Spirits, and they are the ones who are greatly interested in the true evolvement of man to his own destiny. They are part of a vast hierarchy that have a great love for all of God's manifestations, and are constantly with us, unseen forces helping to shape the divine destiny of the planet, our solar system, our Universe.

Come then, and let us explore the first kingdom in nature, the mineral kingdom, and discover a little of the unity in all things.

Cosmic Relationships

Since earliest recorded history man has held an affinity with stones, whether as priceless gems or semi-precious stones used as talismans, amulets or ornamental decoration. They are referred to in the sacred books, both contemporary and ancient, and within the Christian religion of the Western world, specific references are made to them in both the Old and the New Testament of the Holy Bible. And yet, scarcely any knowledge has been brought to light regarding their use or true value other than in a materialistic manner. All we really have available to us is a list of "birth stones," and there is such a disparity in this regard, both as to the proper stone for a particular month and the reason for its use, that it is of value only in a very general sense.

What we are going to cover in the chapters ahead, are some of the true values of various stones, their use and application in the present day, and in the case of some, their prophesized future use in the years ahead.

You may well ask, even as we did, "How can a stone, an inanimate object, have any spiritual value or influence upon mortal man?" This is a legitimate question, and it is only necessary to recognize and understand the meaning of one word; manifestation. All that IS, is a manifestation of God, whether we recognize it as solid, liquid, gaseous, heat, cold, dense or etheric. Everything is atomic, everything is composed of atoms of energy, and there is CONSCIOUSNESS INHERENT IN ALL FORMS OF LIFE, however minute and simple that consciousness might be.

5

Within our current thinking, we retain the concept of separateness, of individual isolation, of being "an island unto ourselves," and yet, EVERYTHING, every form, every organism within ALL forms, all aspects of manifested life in EVERY kingdom in nature are intimately related to each other, even unto our solar system, our galaxy, our Universe. We are ONE!

To consider this principle, let us go back to the beginning of time, when the fiat rang forth, "Let there be LIGHT!" That one word, LIGHT, is the secret to unravelling all of the mysteries of the universe of God, if we can but grasp its true meaning. Let us look at it in its simplest form. Light is ALL THERE IS, radiating out from the God-head, and we recognize that it has two basic aspects to its nature, these aspects generally described as "positive and negative." Light as WE know and recognize it, flows forth from the Sun, and is differentiated by science from the One Light; yet make no mistake about it, when all light, heat, energy, sound, color, vibration and other manifestations are reduced to their lowest common denominator, it is still the Light of the ONE.

Since we work within the lower energies of light, let us consider them briefly. Light as we know it, has a vibrational rate, or wave length, and the range of this visible light we recognize as the spectrum, generally ranging in rate from between 4200-6800 wave-lengths in angstrom units. Wave lengths of color longer than our range of vision are referred to as infrared and radio waves, and those shorter than our visual range, as ultra-violet, x-ray or cosmic. If you recognize that visible light involves only a very limited range of the true spectrum, you will note that our five senses are extremely limited in their receiving ability, both as to sound AND color. This is not to say that we do not receive or respond to higher or lower rates of light or energy. We do, but through the more etheric vehicles of the soul.

Now let us return to the ONE Light, streaming forth through the cosmos in its myriad forms. As it manifests into matter, we detect these as atoms, the building blocks of all things. Until recently, science has generally considered the proton, neutron and electrons of the atom as the lowest divisible unit. However, there is now the awareness of separation into even smaller units of energy. For our consideration, let us stop at the atom, whose countless variations make up the structures of "atomic particles," containing a force-field, a rate of vibration and a degree of consciousness. Beyond this it is not necessary to delve, but only to recognize that they are a "reflection" of the One Light, and from this multitudinous variety of atomic structures our Universe is created.

As the atom has an expression of "positive and negative," and is light or energy streaming from the One Source, it has a consciousness, an awareness of "be-ing," and we can define this expression in the term, "I AM." This, of course, would not be consciousness as we know it, but rather an innate knowledge of procreation, knowing that it can reproduce itself. As it IS light or energy, it has a vibrational rate, thus all atoms of the same structure (that is, of the same number of protons, electrons and neutrons in identical arrangement) can be said to be of "like-consciousness."

It is an esoteric law that atomic particles must come into alignment with each other to fulfill their divine plan and as this is done, we have what are termed molecules; combinations of atoms drawn together for a specific purpose. Thus two atoms of hydrogen combined with one atom of oxygen form water, as a very basic illustration. In every particle of matter, in every design of nature there is seen the infinite beauty of this polarity of the positive and negative aspects of God. In the table of elements and precious metals and gems this is particularly noticeable, and yet you can find it in the endless variety of patterns in plant and animal life, conveying to humanity the consciousness of God in all of its aspects.

The biblical term, "As above, so below," refers to the concept of our being but the mircocosm of a greater macrocosm, so that by looking into a microscope we can see in greater detail the pattern that is repeated throughout the Universe, whether seen through our vision or not. Much that is around us, or more accurately, the vast majority of that which is around us, cannot be seen even with the most powerful microscope or telescope known to man. And yet, as woefully inadequate as our five senses are, mankind is beginning to develop a "sixth sense" of intuition, as part of his expanding consciousness. You may recognize this when we delve into the various uses of stones, in discovering that intuitively you may be wearing the proper stone(s) for your greatest benefit at any particular time. You may hear this expressed as "This stone feels comfortable," or "I can't stand to wear this piece of jewelry," intuitively sensing the vibration of that particular crystal form and its effect upon your own energy patterns or aura.

To better understand this relationship between stones and the human vehicle, a study of the esoteric teachings regarding the soul and its manifested bodies on the earth plane is recommended. By esoteric, we are referring to all that does not concern normal form life or the average consciousness of man. Though many refer to the esoteric teachings as the "occult," giving it a mysterious connotation, this notion should be dispelled. Much of the Holy Bible and other religious books are esoteric in nature, and can only be understood in depth when our consciousness is sufficiently raised. We should all be aware that we are fast coming into the New Age of Light, where much understanding of the soul and its four lower bodies will be manifesting within our collective consciousness, and the sooner we seek this understanding, the greater will be our opportunities for advancement.

Let us consider these vehicles briefly. The sheaths of consciousness which surround the soul we call the four lower bodies, the vehicles of the soul's expression and expansion in the plane of matter. We call these vehicles the lower mental body, the emotional or astral body, the etheric or cell memory body and the dense physical body. It is here the soul gains experience in the manipulation of the laws governing time and space, and it is here also, that the soul develops self-mastery.

We live, move and have our being within what appears to be a three-dimensional world in time and space, yet it is an old occult truism that "time and space" exist only as an illusion within our "three-dimensional world;" that TIME is merely a succession of instants and SPACE is a system of associated points, positions of reference in which the soul can measure growth and progress, and relate this growth to specific areas that he can understand. These "succession of instants" are but the registering by the brain in the physical vehicle of passing events. Thus time is merely a concept which involves events, opportunity, the past, the present and the future, the good and the evil within our brain. Within the consciousness of the "High-self," all is in the NOW, always has and always WILL BE!

As we have mentioned, everything is made up of atoms, and even as the minute atom expresses an awareness, a consciousness, so each cell and organ of the physical body has an electrical awareness of its purpose, and each fulfills that purpose without any mental action whatsoever upon the soul which is occupying the physical body. It is a spiritual truth that man could learn the lesson of his own perfection by watching the process of the cell body, for it accomplishes that which needs to be, without any emotion of jealousy, etc., towards other parts or other cells of the body.

Basically, the physical body functions through what are referred to as the endocrine glandular system and the two-fold nervous system, i.e., the cerebro-spinal and the sympathetic nervous system. Through the glands are secreted the hormones into the blood stream, and from there distributed throughout the body as and where needed, while through the nervous system flows the energy that animates the physical body.

This vehicle of consciousness is automatic in its response, reacting to inner impulses and impacts from the outer world, and has no initiatory life of its own; it is simply the vehicle of consciousness upon the physical plane.

The etheric body is considered to be a part of the dense physical body, as it underlies and interpenetrates every atom, cell, nerve and ganglion within the physical body. Often described as the auric field about a person, it can be detected by those with clairvoyant sight. The etheric body is the energy body used by the soul to manipulate the more dense physical vehicle of that soul. Its function is to receive energy impulses or streams of force emanating from any or all of the seven planes or octaves of consciousness with which the soul is involved, and to transmit these energies into the physical vehicle through the seven major centers of the etheric body that overlie the physical endocrine glands. Based upon the quality and quantity of this energy flow will be the resultant adequate or inadequate functioning of the physical body.

The emotional body is the agent of the soul that works and responds to vibrations from the astral plane of consciousness, and in turn, transmits them through the etheric body to the physical. It is the most potent force flowing into the physical body at this time and accounts for approximately ninety percent of the energy patterns that the soul works with on its evolutionary journey. The most effective way to strengthen and enhance this body is through the use of meditation on a regular basis.

The lower mental body or lower mind, comprises all the knowledge available to those whose consciousness does not transcend the illusions of the material world. We have a higher mind of Spirit representing the field of knowledge open to those whose consciousness reaches to the planes of spiritual reality. However, the soul, in its growth upon the earth plane, will usually focus through the lower, concrete mind that functions in our three-dimensional world of matter or form.

These four lower bodies of the soul we can refer to as our "consciousness," which is, in reality, our spiritual awareness of Being, and this consciousness of "self" needs to be recognized as God in us! Our whole reason for being is to gradually pass through the millions of years of physical sensing into our ultimate goal of spiritual knowing. We have now reached a transition point in our unfolding where we must have that knowing, and we can acquire that knowing only through greater awareness of the Light of the universal Self, which centers us as One with that Light, the Light of God.

However you may wish to use the term, "God," the Creator IS the One Being, the One Mind, the One Life, the One Power, the One Reality.

Let us now journey into the concrete, material and substance world of the Mineral Kingdom, and see how we can employ the various stones to aid us in our attunement with this kingdom in nature, as well as attuning our own four lower bodies with the High Self.

Introduction to
The Mineral Kingdom

Inherent in all life or substance is its relationship to the ONE Life, the Life we refer to in the western world as God. All things, visible and invisible, are merely an expression of that Life. If we are finely attuned to this Consciousness, we can feel it within our own "inner-being" as we gaze into a breathtaking sunset, take in the majestic grandeur of a mountain range, the softly falling snow, in the birth of a new life.

All kingdoms in nature have their own particular expression of that One Life, and within the mineral kingdom, this is very aptly expressed through the myriad varieties and colors of crystals and gem stones. As in all things, there is the exoteric side and there is the esoteric side, (material-spiritual) within this kingdom. The physical or material side is expressed through the many varieties, sizes and shapes of the crystal formations. The spiritual side is expressed through the inner geometric construction that makes up the crystal form.

The study of crystals falls under the heading of crystallography, and when properly pursued is a detailed and painstaking study of geometric and atomic structures. The earnest seeker can find many books on this subject that deal with it in length; our intent is to present to you a small window to peer into, that you may sense the orderliness of this kingdom in nature.

Within the study of crystallography we find there are seven basic crystal categories in which all crystals can be classified, and they are categorized as follows: cubic, hexagonal, tetragonal, orthorhombic, monoclinic, triclinic, and trigonal. The trigonal classification is often considered as being part of the hexagonal system. However, its delineation as a separate system is compatible with the makeup and structure within other planes of matter, such as the chakra centers in the etheric vehicle. These crystal categories are more definitively described as follows:

(1) CUBIC—A crystal in which the three axes are of equal length and at right angles to one another. A prime example of this would be ordinary table salt and crystals of galena, pyrite and garnet.

(2) HEXAGONAL—A crystal having three equal axes at 120 degree angles arranged in one plane, and having one more axis of a different length at right angles to the other three. Beryl and apatite crystals are good examples of this category.

(3) TETRAGONAL—A crystal having two axes of equal length and the third axis unequal, all three axes being at right angles to each other. Zircon is a good example of the tetragonal system.

(4) ORTHORHOMBIC—A crystal with three axes all at right angles, but all of different length. Olivine and staurolite or "cross-stone" are good examples of this.

(5) MONOCLINIC—A crystal with three unequal axes, two of which are not at right angles. The third axis makes a right angle to the plane of the other two. An example of this system would be found in gypsum, epidote and mica.

(6) TRICLINIC—This system of crystal has three unequal axes, none of which forms a right angle with any other. Rhodonite and feldspar are examples of the triclinic system.

(7) TRIGONAL—This system uses the same pattern as the hexagonal. However, the main axis has three-fold symmetry only. For this reason it is sometimes classified as a sub-system of the hexagonal, and is at times referred to as the rhombohedral system. Tourmaline and corundum are examples of this system.

Summed up in its simplest form, it can be said that a crystal form is a visible sign of the molecular arrangement identifying the particular subplane of the mineral kingdom from whence **its** atoms are derived. In the following chapter we will touch on these subplanes in a very general manner, giving you a glimpse into the states of consciousness of their particular atoms. This will give you a little insight into the energy patterns of the various crystal forms, and help you to better relate a particular stone to its crystal matrix.

The atoms making up a crystal have a very orderly inner-geometrical arrangement which gives it its crystalline shape, the many faces or planes of the crystal merely reflecting this internal atomic arrangement. Sometimes crystals are minute, sometimes very large, depending upon how often the internal pattern can repeat itself. This generally depends upon the supply of material available and the availability of room for their growth. It should be noted that well-defined crystals aren't always available to identify a particular mineral. However, this is of little consequence except from an aesthetic sense, as their internal structure remains identical.

Let us now consider the spiritual aspects of these crystal structures. If you will accept the premise that every atom has a state of consciousness, an awareness of its purpose, its being, you will recognize that when atoms of "like-consciousness" come together and coalesce, (as in a crystal form) you then have a body of energy expressing a definite vibrational pattern that has a correspondence or relationship to other

sub-planes in other kingdoms in nature, much as the relationships between the musical scales from A to G. We call this the
"Law of Attraction," which gathers together the atoms of like
vibration or structure, those which can vibrate together in
unison, thus producing a form or an aggregation of atoms.

The principle of the etheric body enveloping and inter-
penetrating the physical body holds true also within the
mineral kingdom, and it is through this etheric body that
energy radiates from or is absorbed into the stone. A prime
example of the radiating principle can be found in uranium
ore, while at the opposite end of the spectrum you have the
properties of lead which have the ability to absorb.

Have you ever wondered why there is such a diversity of
gems and minerals upon this planet? Could it be there is an
endless process of form-building that goes on (as in all kingdoms in nature,) whose basic purpose is the development of
quality and the expansion of the consciousness? In considering these atoms of mineral substance, can there be an
expression of "consciousness" within their corresponding kingdoms in nature? And if so, can we then begin to faintly
perceive the concept that our solar system is but the aggre-
gate of **all** forms, and the body of a Being who is expressing
Himself through it, utilizing it in order to work out a definite
purpose and central idea? If you will recall the esoteric truism
that "we are but the microcosm of a greater macrocosm,"
and recognize that the tiny atom is within itself a solar system
of expression, differing from other atoms according to the
number and the arrangement of the electrons around the
central charge, you can perceive that this theme is being
repeated over and over again in countless forms and expres-
sions, and recognize that we are ALL a part of the ONE
WHOLE.

Let us now look in on the mineral kingdom, and obtain a
greater insight into some of the diverse workings of nature.

Bear in mind that this information was all received from the spiritual side of life through an excellent channel; there was no compilation of data from technical publications on gem stones used to "build" the answers.

The information following was derived through extensive question-answer sessions, editing only when necessary for brevity or sentence structure, and finally, removing all questions from the text that could be done and still retain clarity. While this eliminated the reader's awareness of how the data was gained, the information received remains intact. Should you find that some of the data causes you to question, try to seek deep within your consciousness for the answer. It CAN BE DONE, and YOU may be able to reach into this level of knowledge yourself.

Note: The diagrams below will give a better visual presentation of the various basic crystal formations.

1. The cubic system, with three equal axes (a_1, a_2, a_3), arranged normal to each other;

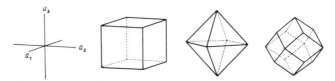

2. The hexagonal system with four axes, three of which are arranged in one plane at 120° angles to each other. The main axis (c-axis) is normal to these three; it is an axis of six-fold symmetry;

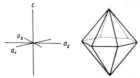

3. The tetragonal system having two equal axes at 90° to each other (a_1 and a_2), and normal to these the main axis with fourfold symmetry.

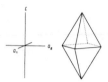

4. The orthorhombic system, with three unique axes a, b, and c, at 90° to each other.

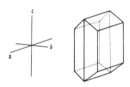

5. The monoclinic system having three unequal axes a, b, and c at an obtuse angle to each other; b is normal to the plane formed by a and c.

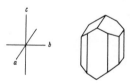

6. The triclinic system having three axes of unequal length (a, b and c), all at obtuse angles to each other.

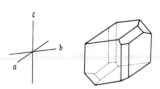

7. The trigonal system using the same pattern as the hexog-onal system. The main axis, however, has threefold sym-metry only.

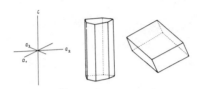

The Seven Crystal Systems

With few exceptions, all minerals will crystallize within one of the seven basic crystal systems, (a notable exception being the opal, which is amorphous,—without shape) and therefore each system, obeying the Law of Attraction, gathers together those atoms which can vibrate together in unison and harmony, producing a form, a crystal, an aggregation of atoms.

Is it possible that each crystal system gets its atoms from its particular sub-plane of the mineral kingdom?

Yes. It gets the atoms from the form of a pattern, but does not draw the energy from there; only the pattern that causes it to come into being, for the sub-plane is much as a thought-form or thought-pattern and cannot give substance, only direction. It causes the correct balance of atoms to come forth to form that which is the pattern.

Can we conclude then, that all stones of the cubic system, as an example, might be expected to have like aspects to their nature?

Very similar. The variations are there, but they are slight. Just as you are able to read an algebraic computation and make certain deductions, so by looking at these particular forms or patterns, you will be able to know what their properties are, for they are very similar, and yet there needs to be a difference, or there would not be the need for other forms.

THE CUBIC SYSTEM

Stones in this category are of a very fundamental or basic nature; things oriented with the earth-plane; bulky problems; ideas or things of a cumbersome nature.

This system corresponds to the sacral center in the human kingdom, and its Ray color is cobalt-blue.

THE HEXAGONAL SYSTEM

These crystals are of a more complex form, and yet they are still rather simple in their composition. They are able to spin off the vitality that is necessary to help other forms of life; they are of a giving rather than a receiving nature. They do not cause disturbances or destructive forces to be given off.

There is also a finer definition with this system, one which causes them to "give off" into more defined areas of being than the cubic crystals. The qualities are of an inquiring nature. They seek into something before they move in. They have the aspect of encouraging growth of other properties, or encouraging other things to come forth.

This classification relates to the solar plexus center in the human vehicle, and corresponds to the green Ray.

THE TETRAGONAL SYSTEM

The basic aspect of the tetragonal crystal is "half-giving, half-receiving." It is of a balancing nature. There are qualities of positive and negative with its formations, as it is able to receive unto itself many of the negative qualities of the earth, and yet it is also able to give forth positive vibrations. The negative is transmuted within it and not returned to the

earth as a negative force or process. Stones under this classification could be considered "transmuting stones."

The tetragonal system relates to the pink Ray and corresponds to the heart center in the human. This is the reason
that it is of a balancing nature. Even as many things might
appear to be as punishment or teaching in the mental plane,
so there can also be balancing. This is to say that all things
which are of a teaching nature are not necessarily negative,
although they would appear many times to be harsh.

THE ORTHORHOMBIC SYSTEM

These crystals have the aspect of encircling, encompassing,
incasing. They are able to surround "energy patterns," problems, and encase them, rather than to disperse the energy.
Orthorhombic crystals are able to isolate problems and to
contain them until they are able to be worked with. This is a
necessary factor in many problems, for often they should not
be dissolved or transmuted until they have been thoroughly
understood and brought under control. Once a particular
problem *has* been thoroughly understood, however, it is well
if it can then be dispersed or dispensed with.

Besides the aspect of "encompassing a problem," it also
acts as a guard or protection, for even as things are encompassed and encased, so can they also be protected from outside, destructive forces until they have been able to complete
their cycle.

This system corresponds to the orange Ray and relates to
the Will center within the human, the center which also has
the ability to accept or reject. Of importance here is for mankind to know that even with "rejection," it is dealing with
the particular problem. The "will" is extremely important,
and you should know that *this aspect appears not only in the
human, but even within other forms of earth matter.*

THE MONOCLINIC SYSTEM

These crystals have a pulsating action. They are able to pulsate with the Universe and to be of a nature which expands and contracts. They are able to reach out and withdraw. There is a growth process with this system of crystal; they expand, reach a point where they break off, and expand again; they do not stay contained. This is a vibration that is important to all mankind and all earth life. Know that it must be continually pulsating, even as that which is considered love or God, is also continually pulsating, expanding, withdrawing, moving and BEING! This is a group of crystals that is most important to all of the cycles of the Universe, for without this, nothing would be accomplished or completed.

The monoclinic system corresponds to the blue-violet Ray, and relates to the third-eye center in the human.

THE TRICLINIC SYSTEM

These crystals have the aspect of completion within their formula. They are considered that which is total within itself; they do not rely on other forms of life or other sources. They are "totality!" The triclinic crystals are complete because the triad formation is reflected against itself; whatever flows in glances back to the center, so nothing is lost or changed. It is continually bouncing off and reflecting.

This system of crystal corresponds to the highest center within the human, the crown chakra, and relates to the yellow Ray. With this particular aspect there is the highest form of understanding, of giving, of receiving, of doing, of being, and through this can all things be accomplished and be made whole. This is the ultimate.

THE TRIGONAL SYSTEM

This form of crystal gives off energy, and does not absorb or receive in any part; spinning, motion! They are neither positive nor negative, but are of a balanced nature. They are constant, continuous movement; there is no need for re-energizing, for they *"are!"* There is no need to break them down or have them react with other things.

The trigonal system is similar to the hexagonal crystal, and although they are the same within their scope, their purposes are varied, the trigonal being of a more strict definition, of a "more purposeful" aspect, of sharper clarity. Those of the hexagonal are more giving and receiving; softer, not as demanding.

The trigonal system relates to the red Ray and corresponds to the very important base chakra (kundalini) within the human. It is all-important, all-encompassing, complete within itself.

Before terminating this aspect of gem stones, let us consider one thing more. You stated that crystal "pattern" comes from the various sub-planes of the mineral kingdom, but that the energy comes presumably from the "God-force." How is it, then, that a particular crystal formation such as the hexagon, as an example, can transmute or send out negative energy, if the energy comes from another area than the sub-plane of the crystal?

The angles and algebraic formulas involved in this particular shape are that which is important to the lesson that it teaches or the work that is done, for even as *all* things are "Love," so are all things mathematically sound.

As man is able to study these particular systems and relate them unto himself, he will more clearly see the workings of his *own* mind and body, and his own place within the universe. It is important to relate to the most simple of all forms, for in doing so, it will appear more clearly what the function of each is, and by doing this, man will then be able to see the more intricate parts of his own being and be able to relate these areas to their purpose also.

The Breastplate

One of the earliest uses of stones (within recorded history) was of a spiritual nature, and was employed by those referred to as "High priests." The breastplate of the High priest has long been a mystery to the average lay-person studying theology, and little wonder, considering the many different stones described as having been affixed to the plate, and the complete lack of information as to why they were worn or to what purpose they were employed.

In researching the Holy Bible, you will find it contains three lists of gems. The first of these is an account of the jewels on the "ephod" of Aaron (Exodus xxviii, 6, 12, 29.) The ephod has been described as having a front part and a back fastened at each shoulder with an onyx mounted in gold and engraved with the names of the children of Israel. The breastplate was made of the same material as the ephod, and folded so as to form a kind of a pouch in which the Urim and Thummin were placed (Exodus xxxix, 9.) The external part of this gorget, or "breastplate of judgment," was set with four rows of gems, three in each row, each stone set in a golden socket and having engraved upon it the name of one of the twelve tribes of Israel (Exodus xxviii, 17-20). The final list of stones is described in Revelations xxi, 19-20.

Ambiguity has existed over the years as to the actual stones used in the breastplate, due to translation from Hebrew to Greek, and later, in many instances, the equivalent of the biblical names of gems is uncertain in the nomenclature of modern minerology, and as a consequence there are several distinct lists of names given for the stones on the breastplate.

To avoid confusion, only the stones of the silver breastplate employed as an ornament for the manuscript copy of the Torah, used in an ancient synagogue, will be mentioned, along with their tribes as follows:

Sard - Reuben	Amethyst - Gad	Emerald - Judah
Agate - Naphthali	Jasper - Benjamin	Topaz - Dan
Chrysolite - Simeon	Onyx - Joseph	Sapphire - Issachar
Garnet - Levi	Beryl - Asher	Diamond - Zebulon

The sapphire mentioned above, was believed to be the original name for the present day "lapis-lazuli," as one example of the confusion and ambiguity that exists. And the stone "sard" or "sardius," is not currently in the nomenclature of identifiable stones.

The stones listed above will be covered within the book in their alphabetical order. We will, under this heading, merely seek to find out a little bit about the breastplate and its use.

What were the breastplates with the many stones on them, used for?

There was the knowledge at that time, of the value of the stones. There was the need for each one wearing it, to be blessed by the breastplate, and also by each of the vibrations that were contained within the stones. Those who wore the breastplates knew the value of these for not only protection, but for the added intuition, insight, healing quality, etc., that could be given through these stones. It was necessary for them to wear this total plate at all times, for through it they were not only protected but able to give wisdom and healing whenever called upon.

The breastplate was used as a form of communication also. There was a deeply hidden language or code that went with it, on a person-to-person basis. Those who were able to wear it used it as a secret language, a secret code, not only a surface quality, but a hidden, symbolic one. They would reveal to each other as they used or pointed at the various stones on the plate.

There was also an importance in the order in which the stones were placed upon the breastplate, although the order and placement were not important to the powers given that particular stone. The stones were arranged in three vertical rows of four stones each, starting on the upper, right-hand side of the breastplate. Note: The proper order described is as indicated on the previous page.

Would you delineate the stones on the breastplate and describe their qualities and use?

SARD

There is really not a present-day stone of equal quality that could be compared with sard or sardius, although carnelian would be its closest counterpart. The sardius stones employed in the breastplates have not been in use nor available since the times of early dawning history. The stone came from a greater depth beneath the earth's crust than chalcedony, and subsequent earth-changes have caused this stone to vanish from the planet's surface.

Sardius was used in elevating the vibrations of the seeker. It would cause a clarity of consciousness for one who is in need. It would help them to define that which they sought.

AGATE

The agate was used to specify the physical need of the person. Through this they were able to divine what was wrong with the party and know what was needed to correct it. It was of a very physical nature and was used many times in their health ritual.

The agate would not be used in this manner today. In the early days of mankind's development, many illnesses were not defined or named, while today there are many different remedies for more specific purposes. Also, those who had the ability to perceive the illnesses are no longer with you. Although there are a few upon the earth who would be able to use this stone in the manner which has been described here, they are a slight handful. This is not a gift that can be taught or learned. It has to be something which is intuited.

CHRYSOLITE

The chrysolite was used to gaze upon or to look into, much as one would use a crystal ball at later times. It was more a stone of focus rather than a vibration that was essential to things. It was used by the priest as a focal point.

GARNET

The garnet was used for words of truth or clarity, thoughts and ideas that would project to the wearer of the breastplate. These were the images of truth! Sharp and clear; strong! The garnet would aid the priest in receiving those visions of truth from the person he might be working with.

There is a quality of perception which goes with the garnet that aids and attunes to the higher vibratory rate of the mind of the giver and the receiver.

AMETHYST

The amethyst was used for healing of a spiritual nature to those of that particular time. This was a stone which was representative of the royalty, and yet, even at that point, they considered the royalty of mankind, though not in their conscious state were they able to grasp the fact that man could become a spiritual king. The amethyst was to increase their spiritual awareness.

The etheric quality of the amethyst has been growing in the past decade and century, and now there is an even greater wisdom and knowledge which would come with the use of this stone, for man is now coming into his own true awareness or spiritual livelihood. The capacity of the amethyst has increased through the centuries, rather than diminished in its use. Note: For a greater understanding of the above statement, one needs to recognize the role of the Seven Rays as they influence the energy forces that are at work on the earth-plane. At this time in the planet's history the Violet Ray, the ray of Idealism, is slowly withdrawing as the dominant energy force, and the Purple Ray is coming into prominence, influencing all those energy patterns of like color and vibration, of like correspondence. For more information on the Seven Rays, read "The Treatise on the Seven Rays" by Alice Bailey.

JASPER

Jasper was the grounding stone, the temple part of the breastplate; it was the stone which caused the wearer to be well rounded and solid in the answers which came through. It was the force which caused him to be able to amalgamate or bring all of the other answers into focus or together.

There was also a quality of balancing with the jasper, for as one answer was given, so was the answer balanced out around it in such a way that the receiver would be more able to understand that which was given.

SARDONYX

This stone, sometimes referred to in error as onyx (due to translation from Hebrew to Greek), was used much as the mirror for seeing within, instead of the crystal, the mirror of vision for the priest. Sardonyx was the stone that he was able to concentrate upon, and from it, his own visions came forth. It was not seeing "in" the stone, but because of his ability to concentrate upon it, it served that purpose.

BERYL

The beryl was the stone which the priest would touch at times when he was faltering in his images; when he was not quite certain of that which came. It was as though he would push or touch this to remember that he had a particular mission in this life and must stay with all truth. This was his form of remembering that he was from the earth, and yet had a mighty mission to perform. This was his touch with reality, to insure that he would remain true to his office. It was much as a grounding wire or grounding stone for him.

EMERALD

The emerald had the force which brought about the wisdom and love that was necessary to translate or transmit all of the thoughts, ideas and visions which came to the priest or the wearer. This was the depth of feeling and beauty; of understanding and co-operation that came to the wearer.

The wisdom of the Priest was also enhanced by the use of

the emerald. Many times he was able to see more than one level of answer as it was coming to or through him. He was able to relate that specific answer to the different areas of the person's life or problems. It was much as tapping several levels of consciousness at one time.

TOPAZ

The topaz was to remind the priest of the earthly beauty of all beings, the clearness of thought and expectation. It was a stone which was used to enhance others, but not particularly to work by itself. Topaz was much as an "added benefit;" it brought to mind the health of the individual.

LAPIS-LAZULI

The lapis stone, (called sapphire in ancient times) was used to enhance the sensitivity of the Priest to the point that he would be far more open to those things which came. It did increase his psychic ability to some degree, and yet the prayer that he indulged in for the greater part of his day was also that which increased his psychic ability; psychic meaning that he was aware of the oneness of his spirit with the outer universe, and that he was receiving his messages from another source other than from within his own being.

The soul that man was aware of at that point is totally different than the soul that man is aware of now. Man knew that he had come from a greater source and Being, yet was not totally aware that he was connected in his *entirety* to that Force or Being, as he is aware today. The meaning of "soul" at that time was somewhat different than it is by today's vernacular.

There was another facet to the lapis of importance to the priest. It was an important measure for man to be able to see himself as others were able to see him, and this helped the priest to be able to relate to each man on his own level. It caused him to have a greater empathy or understanding, a moving into, as it were, of his mind and body and spirit with that one with whom he was working.

The lapis stone has the qualities of causing the spirit to mingle without the body, and to intersperse its own self with other beings.

DIAMOND

The final stone on the breastplate was the diamond. This stone was used as an "ultimate goal," a "truth star," the knowledge of the oneness of the Father over all that were upon the earth. This was the guiding star of Bethlehem to those who wore the star, even though the time was far before the time of the Christ coming into the land of promise. This was their ultimate goal; the seeking for the highest in all of their answers.

The diamond was much as a strong-bladed dagger or knife which was able to cut through to the quick of the problem, to the quick of the answer, to the ultimate goal, so that there was not a shadow of doubt within the mind of the priest or the respondent.

Is there anything of interest regarding the breastplate other than that which was delineated?

The breastplate goes back to the beginning of the "organized church." It goes back to the beginning of man's communion with his God; it goes back to the earliest times of being for man, as far as being able to remember, to the point that he is also able to notice that one stone is different from

another stone; that one man has a belief or a source of knowing other than his own being. It goes back to the time when
man was able to communicate better with feelings than with
words, for his vocabulary, although developed, was not of the
great extent as the feeling coming forth from the stones. It
was much as though one were to touch a prayer-chain or
touch-stone today, knowing that as one does this, they are
better able to relate to the feeling that this gives off, rather
than to put it into words of specific nature.

It should be noted that even though man was not totally
aware of the reasons for using these particular stones, he was
well aware of the vibrations that came from them, and the
fact that they were necessary and needful to his work with his
fellow-man. As he moved on into his own development, he
then became far more aware of the need for these, and the
reasons behind them. However, this was not in the written
form in the beginning, only in the knowledge that was passed
from father to son, and as the ages passed and time developed into a more formal message, then did the meaning of
each of these stones become written or known.

The breastplate was worn, not only as a protection for the
wearer, but as a continued remembrance of the job and the
office which the priest was to fulfill. In touching the different
stones, much as one would touch a rosary today, (if one were
of that particular faith,) the priest was able to immediately
transfer his thoughts and feelings to those particular mean-
ings that the stones held for him. In doing this, he was able
to touch the stone that was of most use to his need, or of the
need of that one with whom he was working. If he were to
remember to remain earthly, he would touch the stone that
ties him in with this particular vibration. If he were to be in
tune with the other person's physical health or his spiritual
well-being, he would touch the stone that to him meant
these particular things. He may not have been able to put this

into words at the time, but he was drawn automatically to that particular vibration that would help and aid or abet him in the job that was to be done. He used this as a form of information, for as he was able to tune to these stones psychically, he was able to give the proper information to the seeker that was with him. He was also able to advise his King, or others on their needs, for he was, again, tapped into these particular sources of information. One who was truly endowed with the gift of his office was much as a spokesman for God, and this was a challenge to each one, knowing that even as today, there are those who are not true to their office, but give because they expect to receive much, or because they are incurring favor of others. This was true even at that time, and many have mis-used this gift.

The priest, in working with another, did not always wait for questions to be asked, but gave forth the information as it was given to him. This is what caused him to be a pure channel, and he was drawn irresistibly to the proper places on his breastplate, for he was aware of the needs of others.

These stones were also as a protection to his own body, for they were able to catch and reflect those things which came towards him as a negative source or form of being. He was not even aware of these, for he had been well-trained in his school, to know that he was continually and purposefully protected from all that was less than good. He *knew* who he was, he knew his particular standing in his community and in the church; he was well aware of his worth and value to all who came.

There were a few who used this as a position of power. Approximately ten percent used it in the wrong manner, tapping the information in a valid manner, but whether they gave out information truthfully or not depended upon whether they actually touched the stone that would call that part of their consciousness forth.

The selection of priests was a part of their birthright, and they were selected from birth onward. Those who were dedicated to the temple were also of a particular tribe, and they were given over in the very early days of their life. They were given as a gift. This is also the reason that there were those who were not true to their office, for even as there are differences in men today, so those who are many times dedicated by their parents are not necessarily those who would care or wish to follow through. This, again, is something that each one needs to learn, and only as individuals dedicate themselves from their own inner sense of being, can they be more fully acceptable to that job which they have chosen.

There were two other items that were used along with the breastplate, Urim and Thummin, and they were contained within pouches on the underside of the breastplate. What was their origin and their use?

Urim was used as an attractor of the more positive qualities or vibrations from within man, for in drawing these forth, the priests were then able to discern the man's needs, knowing those gifts that he had to be able to work with. Urim was able to call forth from the aura of a man or woman, the qualities that could be turned into more aggressive or progressive traits within that particular person, to aid them to battle the conditions which came to them in life. It was necessary for them to be able to recognize these so that they could then be counselled in the wise use of these particular gifts and to help alleviate or master the problems of the day.

The urim stayed inert in the pouch, for there was not the need to use this on the other party, nor to even let them know that the particular condition was there. Only as it attracted or drew forth from people or from the being, was it of benefit. There were occasions when it was necessary for the prist to reach into this pouch and sprinkle some of this ''force'' on the ground unbeknownst to others with him, for in so doing he was able to purify the ground and rid it of all the negative forces which were there. This was only done in very unusual cases, but it could be done, and he had the knowing within him of the time when it was necessary. This was usually when it was necessary to protect a home or a bit of land or to challenge any forces which he felt in the ethers around him.

The urim was worn in the pouch on the right side of the breastplate. It was derived from the root of a particular straw-colored, dry-looking plant that grew in the desert, called thoynosis. It was ground to a powder and placed in the pouch. This plant is still growing in some areas of the world; there is a great quantity of it in the harder to reach places, however it is not of a great benefit today, as man has learned to control his mind and to be able to use these powers without the additional powers of herbs and teas. Man is able to go within, for he now has the knowledge that man in earlier times had, but could not define in language or words. It is not necessary to use these particular herbs today.

The thummin was a disruptive force, one which caused the person to be slightly confused, and yet would jumble their emotions and thoughts to the point that they were able to be "disassociated" from their true inner knowing. Thummin has a power over the psychic body or nature, and is not of a particular physical quality. It works much as a "grader" or screen that would jumble pebbles so that various sizes would fall into their particular size hole.

Unlike the herb, urim, thummin was ground from the marrow of the bones of animals.

Although the term, "disruptive force" is used, it is not in the same context a person might normally use it. Even as it is necessary to plow the ground before one can reap a harvest, it was necessary many times to jumble the emotions and be able to pick out from the things which came forth, the necessary elements of truth, that they might be healed or worked with, and thus it would be much like the "breaking up of the ground." It had the added benefit of healing of the mind and body.

With this brief introduction into how and why the High Priests used the various stones to help others, let us proceed to examine the many facets or energy patterns of the individualized gems and stones, remembering that all things are composed of minute, atomic particles, having an energy pattern and a correspondence to all other kingdoms in nature, and this relationship is there because of ONE THING: we are ALL a part of the ONE! It is necessary for mankind to comprehend this with the innermost part of his being; that ALL are part of the ONE, and one is part of the ALL, and there is a pattern and reason for all things. Nothing is of itself, separate and apart. Be aware of this in all of your thinking and doing, in your reading and learning.

GEM STONES
Precious and Semi-Precious

Agate

Agate is a common stone indigenous to many parts of the planet. A variety of chalcedony, it ranges the spectrum in both color and hue, usually found in varigated, translucent colors with banded patterns.

What are some of the attributes of agate?

SPIRITUAL

Agate has the qualities of blending or binding together the many qualities of man; the ability of tapping several of the chakra centers at one time. It causes the throat, heart and solar plexus centers to meld or work together. Agate calls forth the earthy qualities of man, not to enhance them, but to blend them together. It has the interesting ability of defining truth or helping to bring it out. As used by the High Priests with their spiritual attunement, it usually indicated an affirmative answer or truth.

Agate is fairly complete; it is very subtle in its force, and not of a strong nature, but it does have the effect of giving all things a mellowed aspect, so that they are able to blend and work together. This is a stone that all people can use to advantage. It can be worn in a ring or in a form of body adornment, and it will not be of a negative aspect.

· HEALING

Agate can be beneficial in the area of the stomach, particularly when it feels upset. It would be used in this manner by holding the stone over the solar plexus center to relieve physical discomfort. It would have no effect on emotional or mental upsetness.

Agate helps with the emotion of "acceptance," for through this you will find that even though things are of a negative nature, one can learn to accept that particular situation, knowing that it too shall pass away, and other things shall come to take its place.

ENERGY

The agate reverses the flow of energy within the body or center that is upset, much like reversing the poles in a magnet. It corresponds to the planet earth, and its color vibration is in the bluish-turquoise spectrum.

Man must learn to relate to the agate and allow all of the emotions within to churn and mold together, knowing that as he does this, he may have his good days and bad days, his good areas of work and his lower areas of work, but in the melding together of all, it will cause his soul to blend in physical harmony, much as the beautiful, earthy agate.

Amethyst

The amethyst is a variety of quartz, ranging in color from pale violet to a deep purple. Though its economic value has not been great, it has long been prized by royalty down

through the ages and is considered by many to be a regal
stone.

What are the main attributes of the amethyst?

SPIRITUAL

The health, healing and well-being of the *total planet* are
within the capabilities of this stone of great nobility. Encap-
sulated within the core of the amethyst is the vibration of
love; it is that which blends all areas of the body and the
being together. It has the ability to transmute pain into
pleasure, and break into harmony. It has the ability to change
the molecular structure of things. Light of the sun focussed
through the amethyst is also very beneficial, as it then enhances the rays of energies that come from outside the planet.
It can also be directed towards the moon and used in a like
manner, however it should be pointed out that light rays
reflected from the moon affect the emotional and spiritual
bodies, while the sun's rays affect the physical body.

Although the amethyst can be of great benefit to a body,
both in the physical and spiritual sense, it is also important
that the purpose be of a high repute, and that the one who is
working with this particular stone should also be above
reproach, for stones in themselves, though not dead, are only
as a sending and receiving station, and it is necessary that the
energy be of a vital source.

It may be a hard concept for one to grasp, but within *all*
life-forms upon the planet, as they improve their own selves,
their own being, their own blood energies, so each one is able
to think more clearly, more purely, and to send these
thoughts out upon the earth. As this is given to man to
perfect not only himself, but the earth around him, he is able
to do this more surely as he meditates and thinks upon the
amethyst or gets a clear picture of it in his mind. It is the

pureness of thinking that goes along with it that is of the greatest help.

HEALING

The amethyst is effective as a healing stone. However, *any* stone which is to be used in a healing manner, is needful of a sending force behind it, for that which can draw, can also repel.

The aura of the amethyst is extremely important to the physical body on which it is carried, and also on the physical body upon which it is used. It has the ability to draw to or through it the forces which are being directed either mentally or physically to that particular body. By absorbing these forces, much as a sponge would do, it is able to repel those vibrations which the body does not need. Thus, when it is used as a protective stone, it absorbs and retains those energy patterns which are not right or of benefit for that particular body, and will not release them to that body, but only send them back into the ethers or repel them.

This is not to infer that negative forces are sent back into the ethers, but that these energies are sent back where there is at some point in time, a person, a body or a need somewhere that these energies can be of benefit to, recognizing that all things are energy, and thus energy can be utilized in some manner by all things.

When the thought has been placed with and through the amethyst that there is a particular need for that body in question, it will be able to draw those particular vibrations to it, and allow them to focus through and be given to the body. Even as one uses an amethyst to help another being, he should be of pure mind and thought, for the clearer the mind and body of the user is, the greater will be the benefit to the receiver.

The amethyst needs the mind or mental body to work with the stone to be of greatest benefit. One who wears a stone can only be helped if they are willing to draw that vibration into themselves, and even then, it is only helpful on the etheric body. This can only be the opening, the opening given through the amethyst to the higher bodies, and thus they will be made available in such a way that the physical body will then be able to utilize other energy patterns.

The quality of the amethyst is able to purify and amplify all healing rays. If worn by one who is to be a receiver, it would be a focal point for the reception; if worn by one who is to be a healer, it would be that which they need to focalize their thinking on, so that they might direct the energy towards the person to be healed. In this type of situation, it would be well if both the healer and the patient could be wearing these particular stones, for as they do, it works much as a sending and receiving station.

The color, in itself, is a purifying one (violet); one through which many impurities can be filtered out. It works directly on the arteries or blood vessels. Because of its higher vibratory rate, the amethyst is directly connected to the life force of all things, the life force being the blood which flows in and through all human beings and animal forms. Blue is a purifying force in itself, and combined with the red of active energy (which causes violet to emerge,) it is able to differentiate between the right and the wrong, the pure and the unclean. Knowing that the body is able only to use purity in blood *or* life, it then filters out the lesser qualities that are not necessary or helpful to that particular blood.

In working with the blood, the amethyst works through the etheric body, but not through a particular chakra, for only as the amethyst is held over each particular artery or vessel, does it charge or recharge it. It is preferable that the stone be moved about over the body and placed in the area where the problem might be. It is best used when placed near the heart where the blood flows in, rather than where it is forced out through the lungs.

This stone can be extremely helpful in treating the cases of thrombosis or a clot in the vein where it is necessary for the clot to be dissolved, so that it does not cause greater harm to the body, such as the stoppage of the heart. If held over the clot, it would be found that the clot would begin to dissolve and be dispersed in such a manner as to not create a greater hazard for the body. It should be moved "heartward" from wherever it is being used to dissolve a clot. The stone should be used over the artery or main blood vessel and held for a period of ten minutes, and then gently moved towards the heart.

Another interesting aspect of the amethyst is its effect upon the lungs, as they are greatly affected by its color. The conscious knowing of the color is well to breathe into the lungs in a conscious manner. The whole body of man reaches a new level of being when he is able to thoroughly and completely control his mind in such a way as to meditate upon this color with no other thought of *being* or *consciousness* coming through. If one can breathe deeply at this point, it will help to purify the total body. This is something which has been worked with in times past as well as at present. It would be excellent for one to experiment with this and to try it in their own life. It would also be of help to those who have problems of asthma and allergies in their breathing. This technique would also help to control the lung problems of those who are affected by smog. Work with this, and attempt to use it in your own life, and you will see the difference.

ENERGY

The energy pattern of the amethyst has the ability to change the molecular structure of things, in that it causes struggle within the being, of *all* objects of the earth, causing the molecules of one particular vibrational rate to struggle to become better or higher than it is, and in so doing, it causes the molecules of the structure of that particular article, item or being, to rearrange themselves into a clearer, purer form. It has a very high magnetism within its properties that makes the change come about. It causes the other structures to seek to find that which is more compatible to their being, for even though there is a disturbing force here, it causes peace to come.

The amethyst can be used to recharge the energy within the etheric body by holding the stone over the head, letting the light from the sun focus through it to your crown center. This same energy can then be focussed through your "third eye" to the health and healing of others, and is the center you must focus through when working with your own particular stone. This is a technique of value only to "healers," and has the ability to penetrate and seek within the body of another.

There is another technique of using the energies through the "heart center," the center which has the ability to use the "Law of Grace," in healing. Use of the "third eye" center is well in working with broken bones, for example. You can go to the depth of the wound, and it causes it to be healed or mended. With the heart center, there is the flow of the energy pattern of love. There is a soothing, a blending of all matter. There is not the need to know the specific problem, but only to know that wholeness needs to come, and thus it can be, and it will come in a manner which is not necessarily compatible to the mind of man. This is why we say that it comes as a part of the "Law of Grace."

When wearing the amethyst as jewelry or in healing, wear it as close to the heart center as possible, preferably over the heart center, or wear it in a choker.

The amethyst is a stone that each soul would find useful;

they would be able to find a tone or a note that would correspond to this particular color, and if they can tune to this vibration of tone and color, they would find that it could do a great deal for them. It is a softening benefit for those who are hardened in their thoughts or mind. It is an additive to those who are not.

Aquamarine

The aquamarine is a clear stone of the beryl family, generally ranging from a light-blue tint, graduating into the deeper blue-green shades, long treasured by women as decorative adornment.

What are the particular qualities of the aquamarine stone?

SPIRITUAL

The aquamarine is an excellent stone for meditation. It is a stone in which a soul is able to immerse itself and feel the beauty of all nature. There is a lightness about this stone that causes man to see the equality of life; a sense of serenity or peace with it, much as the sea brings peace to many who have troubled souls.

HEALING

The aquamarine does not have a great deal of healing qualities about it, nor is it of great material value. It could be termed healing, even as water is healing or soothing to a soul, and yet it is not of a strong vibratory rate that would strongly influence a person. It affects the thymus gland of the heart center in a manner of softening the opening of this particular center. In this regard, the most suitable place to wear the aquamarine is in a necklace around the throat. When worn in this manner, it should be dropped below the breast bone, or over the thymus gland.

ENERGY

Peace is the quality that emanates from this particular stone, not only to the one who meditates upon it, but to whomever is concentrated upon while meditating "through" the stone. If you project your energy or thoughts into the aquamarine and think of another, it sends peace to that individual's soul. The vibrations of quietude are within the aquamarine, much as a balm upon a wound.

The aquamarine is of an ovarian nature; this, because the cycles of the person using the stone are important, inasmuch as the cycle of life that the particular person is in, causes the aquamarine to come forth with varying degrees of peace or quietude; of perception, of depth of meditation.

It is well for man to learn to contemplate the aquamarine, and be of a similar nature, so that others might see the truth that is within him, seeing the wisdom that is within him, and yet not being overpowering in this in that he tries to pressure his own wisdom or energies and thoughts upon others. It is well to learn to be soft or gentle, and yet have a strength of character, much as the aquamarine; not to be broken easily, and yet not so unyielding as to be harsh with other beings.

Azurite

Azurite is generally of an opaque nature, associated with copper ore, and varies in color from an azure-blue to a very dark blue.

Is there anything of value in azurite that would be of a spiritual nature?

GENERAL

Azurite is a light stone; one which is good for the beginner or neophyte. For anyone in beginning meditation, its lightness of vibration helps that one to be able to meditate better than other stones that have the ability to attune to a soul. It is best worn as a ring on the right hand, although it can as readily be used as a focal point for meditation by holding two pieces of the stone in the hands. Stones approximating the diameter of a silver dollar would be most preferable.

SPIRITUAL

The spiritual qualities of azurite would be of a lightly cleansing or purifying effect. It will not delve to a deep level of a person's being, but it does cause some of the surface irritations and interruptions to be cleared from the mind. This is its only intent. It brings a semblance of peacefulness to a minor part of the mind; a fine attunement or balancing effect.

There is also a love aspect to this stone that is very gentle, very kind, very patient. Although it is light, it can be an additional help to those who need it.

ENERGY

The spleen is comforted by this stone, but azurite does not have a strong vibration to be able to penetrate it. It would have its greatest use in this manner when employed in use or conjunction with other stones. Generally speaking, stones of an orange color can greatly stimulate the spleen, and caution needs to be exercised with this gland; accordingly, azurite, in conjunction with an orange-colored stone (carnelian would be excellent for this) will act as a balancing or soothing vibration, and greater potency can be achieved in this manner than by either one alone. Note: The spleen, through the lydig center, brings in the pranic energy from the ethers into the physical body. Over-stimulation of this area can bring in an over-abundance of energy, causing problems in the physical.

Azurite is the stone for young children, especially young girls, for in so doing, it helps them to be more gentle in their attitudes; more open in their thinking of others, and in general, more healthy in their over-all attitudes. It will not be a total concept for them, for their minds and hearts must be trained, but azurite would be of benefit to them. Note: In working with young children, DO NOT use carnelian or ANY orange stones with azurite.

Azurite is a stone which is as pure as the water which flows on the earth, as pure as the skies above. There are imperfections in this stone, as in many things, and much of its beauty can be found in its imperfections, and the awareness that things which are not perfect, have the potential within them of being perfect.

Bloodstone

The bloodstone, a member of the chalcedony family, is a deep-green stone with bright splotches of red jasper in it, and has long held a prominent role in mystical symbology, particularly in India, where much of it is mined.

What are the particular qualities of the bloodstone?

SPIRITUAL

The qualities of the bloodstone are of a deep nature, and affect the kundalini center. This is a stone that must be used *only* in the hands of one who knows and has already aroused the kundalini, for in the hands of any of a lesser nature or lower state of evolvement, it is dead or dormant.

Those who are able to transmute this energy should use it in a manner of an unset stone, and move it up and down the spine of the person. It stimulates or activates many of the centers, starting at the base chakra.

A stone of a very powerful nature, its stimulation is of a nature that causes energy to move in the right order (for a particular individual) if it is taken from the base of the spine upward. It doesn't stimulate just the base chakra; it sends out or transmits energy patterns that, in turn, stimulate other areas or centers. One who uses this stone with knowledge will sense the correct direction and timing to be used. They should depend entirely on their own intuitive sense in the use of this.

Does this mean that it needs to be used in the hands of an Initiate, Master or an Adept, in order to be able to open the chakra centers of others?

It would be *blocked* as a powerful tool in the hands of anyone less than a Master. For those who are able to define the ability or readiness of an individual, they may then use this to amplify the energy that is within the spinal column of that particular being. They would be able to draw these energies up slowly, as it is ready, much as a thermometer.

The bloodstone is effective in the alignment of the centers, and the etheric and higher spiritual bodies as well, when in the hands of one who is adept at this. As this information is published, there will be those who come forth and desire to be tested; however, this needs to be used *in a frugal manner!*

Those who have reached the stage of evolvement to be able to use this stone in its most effective way, will have passed the time of their *own* growth, in which they need to be aware of the aspects of greed and lust of power over another person, and thus one does not need to truly be afraid of the mis-use of this stone. There will, however, be those who attempt to make a show of being able to use it, and they will be attempting to force their own will upon that of the patient or the one practiced upon.

HEALING

The healing qualities of the bloodstone could be defined as the alignment of the centers, alignment of the being, alignment of the several bodies of the person; the spiritual alignment of many areas which is required for the perfect physical healing to be made manifest. It doesn't work on a specific illness, but it brings everything into line. Although the energy patterns would appear to be dispersing that which is given, it is also acting in the manner which causes these patterns to be energized and drawn together much as a magnet would do with iron filings.

To properly use the bloodstone in healing, it needs to be used outside of any setting, held in the hand. To that one who knows what he is doing, is patient, quiet and thoughtful, he can use the stone in the following manner: place the patient on a table, having them lie prone on their stomach, and holding the stone in the hand, go over each vertebrae in a circular motion, slowly but surely, and it draws the energy up through the spine. This process may have to be repeated many times.

The shape of the stone is important. It should be in an oval shape, flat on the bottom and a shallow cabochon on the top, having twenty-one faceted edges around the edge of the stone. The dimensions should be on a ratio of two-to-one, such as two inches long and one inch wide, or one inch-by-one-half inch, as an example. It is the proportion that is important. The facets are to break up the symmetry of the edge so that it will be more "all-encompassing," and be able to reach many, many points of the body that are in fault. The facets are important and helpful, but it would not diminish the power if they were not there; they will only increase the value to the individual and enhance the usefulness of the stone.

ENERGY

The energy vibrations are of a very slow rate. The qualities are not of a physical nature, and it would be difficult to relate the energy possibilities here, but they are of a rate which is important for the coming together of the various bodies of your "high-self." Do not attempt to judge those things which you do not see. This is on a plane which is not visible to the human eye.

The bloodstone is of a rather dense nature that has many diversified uses in the hands of a Master or Adept. It will be *a stone of prominence in years to come.* Although it is not a stone of great material value, yet it has an important place in the coming world.

Even as the bloodstone appears to be a common stone, it is only in the eyes of the beholder. You will find that many of the things which have been considered to be common in the past, will be valuable in the future. Even such things as the air, which is common to most of man, *will be very valuable in the future.* You will also find that many of the things which have been placed before you as useless, will come into their own as time goes by.

It is wise never to place monetary value above all else. Many of the materials of the earth are necessary to the sustenance of life. The things which are very basic to nature and to man are the most important of his possessions.

Carnelian

Carnelian is a translucent-to-clear chalcedony, generally red-to-orange in color and occasionally into shades of brown. It has been considered by historians as the stone referred to as sardius in the Holy Bible, (Revelations XXI, 20) and the stone in the breastplate called odem or sard.

How would you describe the qualities that are contained within this stone?

SPIRITUAL

There is a quality with this stone that might be described as "impatience." This might be considered a negative quality or vibration, but it isn't. The carnelian is an excellent stone for someone that is languid, too easy-going, too lazy, etc. They could benefit by this stone because it causes an impatience, an activity that brings about not necessarily more energy, but a stimulation of curiosity. It puts the wearer on the verge of activity, on the verge of follow-through, much as prodding them to become a "do-er." It is a necessary impetus for the beginner.

HEALING

Carnelian is an aid in removing lethargy. It is not a stone to be used on someone who is already of an active nature, but only where there is a need to stir or stimulate.

It can be very useful in the stimulation of the liver, in particular, as it has the ability to cause the liver to throw off some of its own impurities. To do this, you would use the carnelian as a massaging stone, placing it in the hand and massaging it over the area of the liver.

ENERGY

Carnelian is not an energy in itself; it is only able to cause a release within the person so that energy might be focussed toward them. They will still have the need of outside energies to come forth. This is the stone which will stimulate their interest or cause them to be impatient or begin to reach out. In this regard, it can be termed a "beginning stone," the "door-opener," having an effect on the kundalini center. It is not the force that opens the kundalini or cause it to go into action, but it does cause a restlessness within this most important center of the etheric body, helping to stimulate the interest or activity.

The best place to wear the carnelian would be over the throat center or over the third eye. You could also use the stone in meditation, especially if you were desirous to work on the kundalini force. Note: Attempts to arouse the kundalini force without trained, spiritual teachers can be both dangerous AND painful!

The carnelian should remind man that he must not be content to be the lowest that he is. He must always seek to be higher, more informed, more energetic, more active, more of a seeking nature. He must not be as a lump of clay, but the "winged creature that exalts over death." Again, this stone should remind man always, that the divine discontent is essential to the system. He must learn to work with it in such a way that it does not destroy him, nor cause him to be totally discontent, but only to be constantly seeking and searching, without letting it become a fetish with him.

Chalcedony

Chalcedony is a "root" stone, having many varieties, such as agate, carnelian, onyx, tiger-eye, sardonyx and jasper. The most common chalcedony is gray, but it may be white, brown, black or blue.

What would you describe as the prominent aspects of chalcedony?

SPIRITUAL

Chalcedony is a stone that has the power to act as an insulator for all things. It has the power to cut off negative vibrations and to maintain positive vibrations. It can be used as the liner or insulator for many things and should be worn as a protective plate.

Chalcedony was used in ancient times by the High Priests as the material for a chalice, as it has the ability to retain the vibration of that which was placed within it. There was a silver mold that was to go within the chalice, and holy water placed within it would be retained in its original purity, as chalcedony has the ability to maintain and hold the vibration, much as lead shielding can retain or contain the radiations or vibrations of x-rays or atomic energy. The silver lining would hold the vibration and the chalcedony would act as an atomic chamber around it, maintaining the energy within the chalice so that it wouldn't be dissipated.

A chalice made in this manner would be an excellent form of material to hold "holy-water," or water that has been blessed, or water that you place out to receive a blessing. Know that it could then be activated and contained in this particular setting and would be of a more potent or powerful nature than water that is just held within a glass, as the energies will not disperse.

There is no other stone of a similar quality that can be used in this manner. If one were to make a chalice in this way, it would be advisable to place an amethyst within the stem of the chalice, as the amethyst has the power to attract or draw into the chalice. To do this, you would hollow out the stem and place an amethyst within it.

HEALING

Chalcedony is a material that can be used or held over a wound and cause any negative energy from an external area to be repelled or "denied entry." It is much as a protective cover or shield, enforcing an antiseptic attitude for a sore or wound. The stone is of a lasting nature, so that one need not be concerned about having it decontaminated or cleansed, as it has its own cleansing power about it.

There has been much superstition down through the ages about the effectiveness of taking various stones internally, after having them pulverized into a powder. They are but the figment of man's imagination. Chalcedony is *not* to be taken internally, but it could be used in a pocket of a ring or a locket, and in this manner be unobtrusive. This powder could also be worn in a packet or a pouch around the neck or body (or even on clothing) without being of a heavy or restrictive nature. It should *never* be used in contact with living tissue, but only to be employed externally.

ENERGY

Chalcedony has the ability to absorb and repel. It will absorb only that which comes to it, and it can repel anything that comes from an outer source that is not needed at the time. It will absorb, but will not give off. As an example, an energy force can hit it and be deflected, or it can be absorbed;

however, it doesn't absorb it to "give out." The stone does not send out vibrations.

How would the stone know which energy pattern to absorb and which to repel?

This is where the human channel that is working with it is so very important, for only through the vibratory rate of that particular channel can it be energized to accept the forces that are needed or necessary. All energies of a lesser degree are repelled. If the energy pattern is continually raised, anything less than the highest vibration that it is at, will drop away.

Chalcedony could be used over each center or gland as a protective shield at a time when there would be those things which come to that particular area of the body that would be of a negative force, or if there is need to protect that particular center so that others might be developed. It could be used as a shield to keep a particular center from opening. It will not cause a center to close, but it does keep energy deflected from it. As an example, if one were highly emotional, it would be effective for that person to wear a belt buckle with a chalcedony stone upon it (covering the solar-plexus center), or it could also be effective if hung from a long chain around the neck and suspended low enough below the diaphragm to reach the solar-plexus area. When worn as a medallion in this manner, a flat, thin surface of the stone would be used.

There are times in a person's life when he must learn to shield himself against the outer world, even though this might appear to be of a callous nature. Times when he must learn to shield himself from all of the weaknesses of his fellow-man, and the sights of sorrow that he sees about himself. This is not to turn a deaf ear upon these things, but only to cause him to look within and count his blessings over the glories which have already been made his.

This is as chalcedony; this is that which he is holding into himself, and yet shielding from the lesser areas of life, for they will always be there. These are the karma of those who have gone before him, and will continue to go even after him. Those around you bring certain conditions upon themselves, and only through their own growth can they overcome these situations; not because one has great power or pity for them.

Chrysoprase

Chrysoprase is a variety of translucent green chalcedony. Are they quite similar in nature?

Yes, however, chrysoprase is of a more spiritual quality; that which would affect the higher bodies, the top two chakras and the crown chakra in particular. This stone could be employed in the same manner as chalcedony, only on the higher bodies of the individual.

Read the data on chalcedony and apply the same principles to the crown chakra and to the higher bodies of the "self," so that you might be able to define the way which chrysoprase needs to be used. If used in jewelry, chrysoprase need not be on the body in particular; it can be something which is set on the dressing table or is used in any other way, but need not be worn as a piece of jewelry, as the body that it is affecting would not be included in the personal wear.

Chrysoberyl

Chrysoberyl is a stone that is generally yellow in color, ranging into green. The two best known varieties are "cat's-eye," and the more valuable alexandrite, which is emerald green in daylight, and dark red in artificial light.

What are the varying aspects with this stone?

SPIRITUAL

Charity is one of the qualities of consciousness that comes forth with the use of chrysoberyl. It also has some bearing on the heart center, and causes one to be more charitable towards their neighbor, and also towards themselves. It instills within the soul the desire to be more generous with the things which are there; more loving, giving, and forgiving. It evokes a more charitable attitude, causing one to see the good in those things which are around them.

Chrysoberyl has the unique ability to help one "mend their fences," to mend problem areas between their neighbors or their family and themselves. It causes the wearer of the stone to "see the other side," as it were. The stone works on the mental faculties without being an overpowering or strongly forceful stone. It is helpful, a good implement or tool to work with; it is of a supplemental nature. These forces are of a very subtle nature, and might even be denied by one wearing this stone. However, those who are able to perceive more deeply will understand that the work is going on and that it is caused from the reaction or the vibration of this stone in use. This is because chrysoberyl works more on the etheric or mental plane of consciousness; a stone for the spiritual realm.

HEALING

Chrysoberyl has its healing qualities on the emotional (astral) and mental planes, bringing peace to the mind or soul of the person working with the stone. There is no particular body disorder that it would work with; only in the areas where it helps to bring charity into the heart of the person who is wearing it. Of extreme importance here, is being aware that even as one is able to mend the mental and spiritual bodies, this is what lays the groundwork for a more permanent healing in the physical. THAT WHICH MANIFESTS IN THE PHYSICAL, WHETHER IT BE SICKNESS OR HEALING, IS ONLY THE MANIFESTATION OF THAT WHICH HAS TAKEN PLACE ON OTHER LEVELS.

ENERGY

The energy qualities of chrysoberyl are subtle. It has neither the forceful nor the negative pulling energies of some of the other stones; however, it does have a very persistent vibration which works continually. The energy of the stone increases in value as one holds it near or keeps it around. It emanates a soft quality which continues to reach out and enhance the wearer or the one who is working with it. It has a "yeast-like" quality in its energy pattern, in that it continues to expand, rather than just do a job and be done. There is also a luster-like quality with this stone, that which is smooth or satin finished, not brilliant or dazzling.

The energy of chrysoberyl glances off the adrenal glands, subtly enhancing the work that needs to be done by these glands. It does not affect them strongly, nor would it be something that would be detrimental or overly powerful on the adrenals, but rather a slight stimulating effect upon them which enhances the work they do. This would best be done by wearing the stone in your navel or over the solar plexus center for short periods of time. Three or four minutes would be sufficient.

Use the chrysoberyl as needed, knowing that it will accomplish its own job. It is a stone which can be used and then it has a period of being depleted. It is only useful at the time that it is in contact with the body, or is being worn, as it is the interaction of the body with the stone that releases the energy. When laid aside, the stone is cold or mute.

Crystal (Quartz)

The generic name, "quartz," covers a number of stones, such as amethyst, citrine, smoky quartz, aventurine and others. When pure, it is entirely devoid of the faintest trace of color and absolutely water-clear. Such stones are called "rock crystal," and this stone has graced homes throughout the world in carved crystal objects of art, and has also been used extensively as "crystal balls." Quartz crystal possesses the remarkable property of rotating the plane of polarization of a ray of light which is transmitted parallel to the optic axis. Through this property we have long enjoyed the prismatic effect of this stone.

How would you describe the many facets of this stone?
The qualities of the crystal formation (trigonal) are extremely important to mankind and to the universe. You will find that this is a shape which is most universal in nature. It is something which can be made into all other shapes and yet it is the basis of formation that is complete within itself. The formation of the crystal as such, is one of clarity and definition, pureness and depth. It is a formation which teaches many things to mankind, for in gazing upon this and meditating upon the formation, man is then able to see his own

being, for as he looks into the crystal he will see the reflections of many colors, the reflections of many other people; the reflections of his own thoughts. He will also be able to see the brittleness of himself; for even as the crystal which is struck with force shatters into many pieces, each with the same characteristics as the mother piece, so man, as he shatters his own being, will find that fragments of himself fall away that are of the same crystalline force that he is, himself.

The areas within man are ever-changing, much as the colors within the crystal. As such, they are found to be very elusive or difficult to hang on to; difficult to be able to cope with, for he sees them momentarily and they are gone with a flash, much as the prismatic effects of the crystal. It would be excellent if man would continue to peer within himself and constantly seek for these changing attitudes and benefits, at the same time recognizing that they are but flashes of that which can be, and parts of that which *is* to be.

SPIRITUAL

Clearness is the quality which is foremost with this stone. It is part of the eye of the beholder in this instance, working particularly with the third eye. Man needs to look to the area around him; the world, the hemispheres, the Universe. He needs also to look down into the smaller forms of life that are around him; he needs to look within his own thoughts and his own being, for from all of this will he be able to come up with a faint image of that which "IS!"

The total picture is too much for man to be able to conceive, unless it looks like a "nothingness" to him. He must realize that each thing is "all things," and through this he will be able to cope with his life on a "day-to-day" basis, knowing that as he improves one particular area, so is he improving his total area or being. As he is able to make a small amount of progress for his town or city, so he is doing it for all towns and cities. This is the knowledge that he must learn to accept and work with, for whatever is accomplished is not lost, and it becomes magnified as it is multiplied. Note: Threads of philosophy are given by the teachers throughout this book. If you can absorb the above statement into your consciousness, accept it and apply it, much of the underlying purpose of this book will have been accomplished.

HEALING

The healing qualities of crystal are mainly an amplification of the energies of the one working with the stone. It amplifies the abilities of whomever is using the crystal, changing to fit each particular person, and it can be worked with most any illness, because it is only amplifying the energy of that person who is working with it.

Using a crystal in both hands would help to amplify the healing that is flowing through the person. The most suitable method would be to use a pyramid-shaped crystal, holding the pointed end against the palm and the flat side facing outward.

ENERGY

The energy of the crystal varies and is predicated on both the size and the shape of the crystal that is being used. It can be changed and altered and this in itself can be quite an art. The crystal is able to tap the energies of the universe, with or without a particular person working through it or with it, and yet it can be modified by human aura or touch.

Is that why this particular stone is often used in crystal balls?
The energy is important, but it mainly causes man to reach

a point of infinity in which he is able to see all things clearly, for *it is his own mind projecting,* rather than that which he sees in the ball. It is not the crystal itself, but it is the fact that man can reach into this and become "at one" with all things. It works with the third eye in the etheric body.

The crystal can be used by amateurs and professionals alike. It is not something that you would be able to pick up and immediately use, and yet to each person there is a personalized sense of touch with this. It becomes different things for different people according to the need. Knowing this, one can begin to play with, or experiment with it in many, many ways. Find that which is your own particular gift and use it to your highest or ultimate goal. Know that it has an endless variety of uses and purposes, and it is up to man to define these. Be aware also, that a particular size stone at one point in time would not necessarily be adequate at a later period.

When using the crystal in its natural crystal form, it is a good stone for meditating.

The quartz crystal can relate well to the heart center, but it is mainly for the third eye, or that which is of the mind. Those who are able to tune to this are able to work better or more clearly with their mind when they are concentrating upon it. In this regard, it releases the mind, or the third eye, from the concentration upon any one form, thought, color or area. It is a total blankness, and yet it reflects clearly and magnifies that which comes to it. This is not because there is an absence, but because there is an "allness" to this stone.

The crystal also affects the crown chakra. It is quite potent in this area, and must be used with caution in working with this center. It has strong energy vibrations which emanate from it, and these could be of a disruptive nature if one has not overcome the will, for when they have opened this chakra, it must be available to that which comes and not be of a blocking nature. When there is a sense of blocking from the high center it meets the resistance of the crystal, and this causes a painful experience.

Crystal is not a stone you would normally wear. When used in healing, have it strapped onto the hand, palm downward.

Quartz crystal is the mineral that man will find most closely relates to his own life, for even though he is not as perfect as the diamond, nor as valuable as the diamond, (at least in his own eyes,) he could more nearly relate to the crystal, for it *is* of great value; it is of a beneficial nature, not only to his mind and body, but also to his spirit and soul. He would find that it also causes him to remember that he, too, is part of a total number of crystals which are formed in the same manner with the same similar shape, although they are many sizes and are able to reflect many different colors. And as the crystal is not of the same hardness as the diamond, it has a comparable relationship to a man, although man at some future time will develop the strength of character symbolized by the diamond. In his present state of evolution, he is more readily adaptable to the strength of the crystal, and should recognize the value of relating to something which is not colored after any one particular hue or aspect, for then he becomes clouded in his thinking or he may also become more lopsided in his viewpoints. The quartz crystal causes him to be more open and clear, and these are things that he should strive for.

Within this association, crystal represents a great deal of strength or strong vibrations, as far as energy patterns go, which resemble the same within man. Man has the energies of the universe within himself, and it is well that he learn to channel these to a useful purpose, rather than to destructive areas that have been so prevalent in the past.

Diamond

The diamond is the hardest of all gem stones, being considerably harder than the next classification below it, and yet it is composed of pure carbon, which also occupies the opposite end of the "hardness spectrum." It has long been symbolically associated with the marriage ceremony, whether by accident or design.

Is this stone as important spiritually as it is on the material plane?

Yes. It has aspects that cover the whole spectrum of energy, and there is little or nothing that cannot be helped by this particular stone.

SPIRITUAL

There is the adding of "infinity" to the one who wears the diamond; the unending searching or seeking within the soul is amplified by the stone. The balancing of the inner lights, colors or qualities are also present, and there is another aspect, a total openness of being that is symbolized by this stone, that is important to the wearer. Spiritual heights may be attained when one can contemplate the diamond and yet not be aware of, or swayed by its material value. Those who are able to look deep within the diamond and appreciate it strictly for the beauty that is there, for the clear-cut colors, for the depth, for the perception, for all of the beauty and glorious qualities that are there, will receive the greatest benefit from this stone.

HEALING

The healing qualities of the diamond are not of a specific nature. The diamond is a stone that is best used in conjunction with other stones. It is able to amplify and penetrate, and yet it does not work of its own in such a manner. It is the magnifier of the other stones, and is particularly helpful when used in conjunction with the emerald and the amethyst.

ENERGY

The energy of the diamond is that which supplements all physical energy, for as one is able to wear this either as a ring, a broach or a necklace, it enhances the physical energy of that soul. It is of general amplification and use. It is an example of perfection. The diamond is to the soul, what bread is to the body.

The diamond is also an aid in the opening of the two higher centers (the third eye and the crown center.) It can be worn over either of these or both. It is only to attune that particular soul to the higher forces, but does not harm in any manner. It can be worn anywhere on the body and be of help to the wearer.

Are there any additional benefits in the use of the diamond?

Yes, but at present difficult to apply. The diamond could be used in alleviating the pressures in the eyeball that cause glaucoma. This would need to be the blue light that is reflected from within the diamond and played upon the eye, a technique that will not be perfected for some time to come. Glaucoma is the result of a deficiency in the body system; a portion of the carbon content in the body makeup is missing.

This could be detected as a chemical imbalance if there were a more true and accurate testing that could be given to a person as they move through this life experience. It will be able to be done in times of the future, for there will be the *auragraph* or *aurameter* which will detect the imbalances in the body before they are seen even in the blood stream.

Do not doubt that these things shall come to pass. Within the next five years there will be greater discoveries than you can conceive of at this point. Man is upon one of the greatest eras in history, and yet it is also one of the most fragile, for it is a time when many things can break apart and fall asunder. Man needs to be extremely careful with his own being, and in each area that he can raise the vibration even one nth of a degree, he must work to do so, for as he is doing this, he is helping all of that which *is!*

If one were capable of reading the aura then, would the color that was lacking be the color that would need to be added to the aura?

Yes, and this is the area that needs to be perfected before man can locate his illnesses, which are coming upon him in great profusion at this point in time. In the case of glaucoma, this would show up as a flickering, white area in the aura. The body would then realize that there was a need for this added element in the diet and it could be given in such a form as to supplement this, long before the need was actually shown as a weakness in the eyes.

There will be many indications within the aura of imperfections that will be determined over the years, and man will begin to understand and be able to correlate these in such a way as to supplement the diet or the particular need that is lacking. In one case it might be minerals or it might be vitamins; it could be the need for more protein or less of the leafy vegetables; it can be many things, and these are the areas that will be more defined in the aura of man in the times to come. Know that as it is showing in his aura, so it is in the outer bodies and *not yet a part of the denser physical body.* All of this will take time for mankind to be able to comprehend and be able to work with.

One of the important ingredients that will be used in developing an *aurameter* is silicone, which will be employed in reading and registering of the impressions. There is a complete graph that would need to be made and given through the right channel. There are those who have, even now, the concepts of this in their mind, and it shall be brought to pass. Be aware that many of the things which are being done with the photographs of the kirlian photography, will also be additional information to mankind, and there are now those who are beginning to catalogue the different impulses as they come forth from the body. These are not mere happenstances nor accidents, but those things which have been pre-ordained by those of us who would bring enlightenment to mankind. Note: Kirlian photography as presently employed, has not found acceptance within the scientific community. As more valid techniques are developed, the relationships between the various bodies of man will be more apparent.

The primitive forms for these devices are already being formed within the minds of man. It is necessary that he continue to seek within himself and find the answers, for he has caused his own ills and he must come to help find his own salvation. He will one day be able to destroy many of the ills before they become a part of him.

Although the diamond is usually of a clear color, it comes in many colors and hues, and while all are of a similar nature, you will find that they are *the most refined quality* of any of the colors of that particular spectrum, the highest of any. If it is a yellow diamond, for example, it is the highest form of yellow, greater than golden topaz in that particular color. It is the ultimate!

Man, in his own mind, needs to compare himself to the diamond, constantly looking for the colorful facets that are within himself, within his mind, intellect and soul, and as he is able to see these in clarity, (as he would see the clarity of color in the diamond,) then he can begin to see himself becoming a perfected son of God, the Father.

It is necessary that each area of his life be polished and faceted so that it can reflect the beauty that is there, and not be one that absorbs or diminishes from other beings. This is man's true nature; to become "diamond-like" in his qualities of mind and soul.

He needs to transfer his thinking from the crystal to the diamond, for in so doing, he goes from becoming the man of the earth to the Father-image that he has been seeking these many, many eons. He will find this is the perfection which is in his mind and in the eye of the universe. Do not feel that it is unobtainable. Even as a diamond was not built in a matter of years, but took eons of time, so shall man become the perfected being that he seeks after.

Emerald

The most valued member of the beryl family is the emerald, whose deep-green color has long been prized by royalty and commoner alike. It is one of the few gem stones that can be deeply flawed and still retain its value in the eyes of gem lovers.

Does the emerald have the same value spiritually as it does on the material plane?

More so. There are so many facets to this stone as to make it very remarkable and its future potential is unlimited.

The emerald is a "clear conscience." It is of a "like vibration" to that which is within the mind of man; that which causes him to desire to give wisdom and love to others. It has the aspect which causes him to want to think in new depths; it causes him to want to give.

SPIRITUAL

The greatest spiritual aspect with the emerald is the giving of wisdom from the mental plane. Although wisdom cannot technically be "given" as a gift, it is given as a truth within the person, so that they are able to perceive all manner of things with greater wisdom. It has the effect of enhancing the wisdom from the mental plane.

Another of its spiritual aspects is the vibration of love, and it is one of the more important qualities of this stone. Not only the love that is within it, but the love which is projected through it.

HEALING

When the heart has been affected, whether it be of a mental, physical or spiritual problem, the emerald is a strengthener, and it has the adhesive quality that is necessary to draw all components back into a sense of oneness with each other. (This quality is known as love, and yet it is a certain vibratory rate, also.)

The emerald also affects the backbone of the person wearing it. Those who have a tendency toward back trouble will receive strength from it in a physical way. One method would be to place it on the index finger of the left hand. Rub it on your right hand, creating friction, and then place the right hand on the back. The stone draws forth from the right hand some of its own ability or quality. To be used in this manner, the emerald must be free and clear of all adornment, set out and away from the setting of the ring, and yet it should be worn upon the *index* finger of the left hand when worn *as* a ring.

When the ring is brought into direct action or friction with the right hand, it then creates a force which can be used in the healing of the back. Once this friction is created and a glow or warmth is noticed in the right hand, the right hand may then be placed upon the back of the person with the problem, directly over the area of hurt; not rubbed, but merely placed over the area. This may be repeated over and over again as necessary, placed over each particular vertebra, stimulating the nerves within.

The emerald is also quite useful in alleviating the problems associated with sugar diabetes. It can increase the vibratory rate of the body to the point that it is able to fight off the disease of its own. The healing comes from within the body itself, not from the emerald, but the stone does stimulate those areas which will cause the healing to come about. It would take a great deal and a very large stone to help in this manner, but if it were available, it should be held over the solar plexus. While working in this manner, you would also be cleansing the bile duct. The method entails holding the stone between your fingers and let the sunlight (preferably) go through the stone to the person. This works somewhat like yellow jade that is placed on the back of the hand, with the palm of the hand held over the solar plexus center.

The adrenals are also affected by the emerald. They are enhanced and stimulated through the use of this, especially when it is used on the backbone.

In using the stone as a healing device, would it be beneficial if you moved the stone up and down the back of a person's spine?

If one holds the stone between the healing forces of the hand and the part of the back to be worked upon, you will find that the benefit is enhanced. The individual would lie on their stomach and you would hold the stone over their back or spine with the left hand and use the right hand in healing, with your palm facing down. The ring should be held a distance of about two inches above the body, and there should be an additional two-three inches between the stone and the healing hand. This technique would be used for minor adjustments of the spine. It draws the spine into a firm, straight line. It will not correct things that are totally out of line, but it strengthens what is there, because it works on the substance of which the bone is composed. There is also a stimulating effect upon the nerves which are located within the vertebrae of the back. There is a great deal of activity here, and although it would appear to be of a rather subtle nature, it is also of a rather powerful nature.

ENERGY

The emerald strengthens the particular vibrations within the wearer that have been mentioned; it causes the wearer to be more in tune or harmony with those particular qualities. In addition, it can add its vibration to not only the one who is wearing it, but also to a companion. It is somewhat as a bridge between people, as a bridge between thoughts, as a combiner of efforts or forces. It has the qualities of drawing together different aspects and combining them in such a way that they can be a more usable energy when returned to the world. Some of these aspects could be described as strength of being, strength of character, strength of thinking.

This stone, while affecting the glands, has a greater effect upon the centers. It causes each center to feel its own purpose, its own being; in this regard it is most pronounced in the area of the solar plexus, but not *of* the solar plexus.

It should be mentioned that the moon is extremely important in the use of this stone. When the moon is at its fullest point, this is when the greatest benefit may be derived from the emerald. It has a sympathetic quality or communion with the moon, and can be more effectively used in healing when the moon is full. Concentrate on it and work with it. The week prior to the full moon and the week following would be the best time, with the energy peaking at full moon.

The emerald also affects the deep heart center; not the blood in the heart so much, as the muscles that pump the heart. It affects the heart much as the moon affects the tides of the earth. There is a certain pull which goes with this stone that affects the very central part of man, much as the moon causes the oceans to rise and fall.

If you are a healer, and wear the emerald at all times, it would be best worn on the little finger or the ring finger. As a lavalier, wear it down over the heart center (in the ''v'' of the bodice.) It can also be worn in a bracelet on the right arm. If worn on the right arm, this would be the hand that would be used in healing, and it would be beneficial in any other work that you do.

The emerald is not a stone to be worked with constantly, but to be used for specific purposes. Put it on when you desire to use it in a meaningful manner to others.

Man-made, or synthetic emeralds are quite common today. Are they of equal benefit compared to the natural stone?

The vibrations of the man-made stones are helpful, but are *not* as totally beneficial, much as an artificial vitamin is not as easily assimilated by the body as a natural vitamin is. The manmade stones do not have the finest quality of vibration. They are of a more coarse nature; and there are elements that cannot be contained in them that come into the natural stone.

Because of the energy in the natural stone, it is important that it be used only at a time you are specifically or consciously using it; not wearing it constantly on the finger. This is particularly true when wearing the emerald on the *third* finger when working through the heart center, because it then has the tendency of draining the energy from you.

The emerald is the ancient stone which contains within it, waters of healing. Within it also, is contained the beauty of all the ageless wisdom which was first brought into the use of man's paradise, the green paradise, the green planet, which you represent.

Within a stone also, can be the qualities of the giver. The giver and the gift are also involved in a stone's radiation. As a stone is given with love, it reflects and rebounds those same qualities to the recipient. Be aware also, that as a stone is stolen from another, it causes a very negative activity to go on with that same party. Thus, these other areas must also be taken into consideration.

The importance of the emerald to mankind cannot be over-emphasized.

Garnet

The garnet is a stone of many colors and varieties, ranging in color from deep emerald-green through yellow, brown and red. It is the red, translucent pyrope and rhodolite garnets that we are generally acquainted with.

How would you describe the vibrations of this stone?

SPIRITUAL

The garnet is a stone of great depth, of great wonder, of great purity. This is the stone which is needed for the pituitary gland, for as one is able to reflect upon the garnet, the energy or "rate-of-vibration" enters the third eye center and affects the pituitary gland in such a way as to cause it to "stir up from the depth." The garnet has the ability to cause the "all-seeing mind" to reach back into past lives, past incarnations and to seek out the information that is there for the growth or the good of the being that is concerned with this particular aspect of the stone.

To use this technique, the stone should lie on the top of the patient's head that is being helped. The vibration of the stone is then able to free the membranes which bind the thought-forms of that particular person, so that the thought-forms can be freed into the ethers and adjusted in such a way that other persons can see these forms or read them more freely, picking out the details which are necessary for the patient's understanding. The term "membrane" is more of a symbolism, for there is not a physical membrane which holds the memory; however, there is an etheric membrane, and the garnet is able to free this by its energy patterns.

These thoughts can then be re-adjusted in that person's mind so that he will understand the needs, the helps, the hurts, the good that has gone on before. For someone to effectively use this technique, it would be well to carry the stone around in their pocket or in some place that is very close to their body for a period of time. The garnet attunes itself to you, so that when you place it on another's head, there is a closer tie. The thought-forms that are released through this stone are *only those that are necessary and beneficial* to the patient.

HEALING

The solitude, the peace, the quiet, the "depth-of-well-being," can be affected through the use of this stone. The garnet is a stone which can affect the wearer or the one with whom he desires to work, for it is a stone which can have the energy reflected through it to another being.

The garnet has the quality of being a great inspiration during a time of contemplation. In this instance, you would hold it in your hand so it can be felt. The shape of the stone in your hand is of no actual importance. However, concentrate and visualize a garnet that is shaped like a "brilliant-cut" stone (*58 facets*) with a pointed end. Try to recall the *color* of the garnet you are holding, purely and clearly in your mind's eye while visualizing the diamond shape. This helps to attune you beyond all things; it enables you to tune out all interruptions.

The garnet can also be employed as a protective stone when worn over the third eye. In this manner, it will protect you from outside influences and remove from your consciousness the awareness of other people's problems; however, it is not to be considered of a healing nature when used thusly.

To most advantageously use the garnet in healing, hold it over the spleen. It cleanses, purifies, enhances and magnifies. The spleen is an organ which has difficulty in being stimulated properly. There is constantly a residue in the average person that needs to be stirred and cleansed, so that the total system can be more vital. Used this way on a weekly basis would be beneficial to any and every system.

The green garnet has the value of "depth of healing." It needs to be projected through, for this is a purifying stone for the thoughts of man. It is important that man think "towards" this stone; allow himself to be purified. The energy can then be used for the healing of others.

The red garnet represents the depth of love, the depth that is in all things, the depth that is within God. Through this stone, and because of it, many things can be expounded from one person to another. Know that the very visioning into this stone can give the feeling of eternity or eternal love. This stone, working within your consciousness, will cause you to strive to be better than you are, to reach for the perfection that is yours.

ENERGY

The energy quality is that of balance, of peace and solitude; the quality which can round a personality to its fullness.

Different shapes give off different energy patterns. The rectangular stone is of a more mundane nature. It causes things to be in "blocks or sections," or in a particular balance. It does not have the all-encompassing value that a round or circular stone would have. A circular stone with a pointed end is an excellent shape to use, as it can focus directly upon a particular area of the body when used in a healing manner. The square stones are very helpful in business opportunities or business situations or conditions; the rectangular stones are most helpful in those things which are of the earth or of the mental body. The shape, however, is secondary; it is the color and vibration of the stone which are most important. The shape is merely an added benefit, but is not essential. A stone of any shape that is pleasing to the eye can be soothing to the consciousness, and thus it is well to vary the shapes and sizes so that they will not be of a single shape or nature. Be always alert to new thoughts, new ideas, new shapes, new sizes, new colors and figures.

The pituitary gland is affected by the garnet, and also the base gland of the intuitive centers, for it is through this that great depth of projection can come about, knowing that the "silence" of this stone is able to reach great magnitude.

In using the garnet with the base chakra, the person being treated should lie on their stomach and the garnet should be held over the end of their spine (where the tail bone is situated.) It is not necessary to concentrate or think on the stone, but merely to hold it over the area. It has a pulsating action; it stirs and soothes, stirs and soothes. Descriptively, it begins an action and then it soothes it over to refine it, much like you might stir up mud and refine some of the dirt particles out. It would need to be used in a rhythmic way, or over a period of many months. Used in this manner, the garnet can cause a great deal of cleansing to come about within the consciousness of the individual being treated. However, it should only be used with those who are able to continue in their growth and are seeking for the higher levels of learning.

Be patient with this technique of purification, and recognize that you should not use it lightly, for the garnet is indeed a powerful stone and can cause a great deal of trauma for one who is not yet ready for this particular experience. It causes a great deal of "dis-harmony" to come to the particular body being treated; it can be painful; not necessarily of a physical nature, but only of that which causes the person to be very uncomfortable with himself and others.

The story the garnet has to tell man is that he needs to be patient and constant; he needs to be continuous in any action that he starts; he needs to learn the ebb and flow of his own being and to work patiently with it; to give and take with all of his fellowmen. He needs to have the depth of color and feeling; the depth of warmth and empathies that this stone can epitomize in his mind.

The garnet is the symbol of greatest love and compassion, and as he uses it, especially the red one, he needs to think of these same deep qualities within his own soul.

Jade

Jade has been a stone of great prominence for centuries, and has long been a part of oriental philosophy. Within China and Japan, it is considered to be THE most precious of all stones.

The Chinese have credited five cardinal virtues to the qualities of jade: clarity, modesty, courage, justice and wisdom. Jade is actually a general term that properly includes two distinct mineral species, nephrite and jadeite, nephrite being the more common and considerably less-valued than jadeite.

Is jadeite as valuable a stone as the orientals hold it to be?

Yes. Jade in its many shades has many important aspects to its nature.

SPIRITUAL

Jade can be piercing and tranquil at the same time. Piercing, in that it reaches the depth of wisdom within a person, and reaches to the depth of any problem. Tranquil, in that it brings the peace that is necessary *to* that particular problem, for many times, once the problem has been voiced, the answer will also come.

Jade is a good stone for meditation, a good stone to think on, to see, to have within your home, for as you pass it, you will unconsciously tune to its vibration and pick up its quality. It is also an excellent stone to touch or to hold in the hand, for there is such a tenderness and a warmth that emanates from it, that it produces or projects a tranquil sense to that one who is feeling or touching it.

The various colors of jade have within them similar qualities; however, when you use the more colorful stones, (red, orange, etc.) you are addressing certain areas of anger, hate and lust, and when you wear the other colors of greens and blues, these are speaking to the purity, the love, the emotions, the growths, the affections.

HEALING

To be effective as a healing stone, the jade needs to be placed upon the particular area of need. If it is an emotional problem, it is well to first decide the color that you are going to use, and place that near the chakra of the same or corresponding color. In this situation, it is well to use lavender jade if it is at all available, for this color stone has the more tender vibration. Using this technique, you will be able to bring forth the problem in a clearer manner, and also the answer which will come to it. This will be clear, and yet very subtle, for those things which are perceived will not be given in a sharp or harsh manner, but in a very workable way.

ENERGY

Jade has a strong influence on the heart center, and the glands are affected much as a reflection or a ripple. It affects the glands in such a way that it causes them to give up their impurities. It acts much like a magnet, the glands tending to reverberate to the jade, and in so doing, give up their impurities.

Its effect on the heart center has much to do with the flowing of higher rates of energy from the lower centers, through the heart center and on into the higher centers of the etheric body. As the jade is held over the heart center, and the lower energies pass through, they are stirred and purified, thus causing them to be of a refined nature when they reach the higher centers of the body. This causes a great deal of energy to flow upward, energizing the higher chakras. The sapphire, which is more penetrating, is of greater benefit to the physical heart, while the jade is more of a purifying nature. The working together of the two stones could cause a more complete form of purified energy to flow into the other areas of the body.

Since the different colors of jade have different aspects, how would you delineate these?

LAVENDER

Lavender jade radiates love, beauty, security. It is beneficial in the healing of mental problems, or problems connected with the mental body. Worn as a ring on the left ring finger and held over the crown chakra of the one that is mentally upset, would be the most effective way to use this stone. Lavender jade can help to bring about a mending of the emotional and mental bodies also, so that they can work more in attunement with each other.

RED

This color of jade is one which can be of an energetic vibration, and yet it will also bring forth any anger that is within the person. Working with the red jade, there is the sensation of stirring up of emotional problems, and yet it is like stirring up from the bottom, so that sediment rises, (figuratively speaking,) and when it settles, the emotional problem will be of a clearer or better defined nature for the soul to work with, helping them to see and face their problem in a better manner. When used on the ring finger, it will go through the heart and help that person to see what they need to work with or work out. It also gives them the answers to work with. The red jade also has a stimulating effect upon a person, causing what might be termed ''divine discontent'' within the soul.

ORANGE

Energy is the main aspect with the orange jade. It helps a person see or know, or find the causes of their lack of energy. It brings this problem before their sight so that they know how to work to change or reverse "lack of energy" into energy. It nullifies or eradicates apathy.

The spleen is one area where employing orange jade *must be done with great care,* as the spleen area should not be worked with in a casual manner. Many of the aspects of healing are used by man on a part-time or spasmodic basis, which is not good. One should go into these subjects in depth before beginning to play or experiment. It is necessary that you take the total body into consideration when beginning to work with any one organ or chakra. You must also know the condition of the other chakras, or the other areas of the body, because if other areas are also out of balance, this can cause very disruptive things to happen.

YELLOW

The yellow jade works on the solar plexus. It is related to the bile, stimulating it and aiding poor digestion and constipation. It is also of help in working with the solar plexus center, itself. In stimulating the bile, the stone should be placed directly over the area. This particular color of jade should not be worn directly on the body, but kept apart, such as in a purse. In this manner it helps one to defend themselves from outside influences affecting their solar plexus center. They are able to be aware of the energy force but able to keep it apart from them.

When placed on the lower back, even with the hips, it is an aid to the pancreas.

It is well to imagine the piece of jade that is carried in the purse or within the outer garment, so that it is ever before the third eye or the visionary part of the being. This causes them to be able to concentrate upon it, and know that it is with them as a protective force. It has a soothing effect.

BLUE

The blue jade has an effect on anything to do with the head; the mind, the thoughts, the ideas, the imagination, the meditation, the inner workings of the head. It has no effect on any organs or vessels, but only on the intangibles in the head and mind. When working with the mental body, it acts as a filter, and should be worn around the neck.

Blue is the most peaceful of the many varieties of jade; this is the one which can be used with very little problem, for all people are in need of being able to assimilate its effects upon their bodies. This stone can in no way over-stimulate or cause a person to over-react; it can always be given safely as a gift and be used by anyone.

SALMON

Salmon jade influences the adrenal glands. It has a stimulating effect upon them, but once again, it must be used with care, recognizing that only if these glands need to be stimulated, should this be done.

CREAM

Cream jade is neutral in its effects, carrying the general qualities that are a part of the energy pattern of all jade. Nice for carving or focal points of beauty, but not of a particular nature.

MAUVE

Mauve jade is much like the cream jade, however it is spiritual in quality, spiritual in nature and spiritual in development, having a very delicate vibration. It helps one to focus within and find their own spiritual need; finding that which needs to be added or taken away from their own personality, to cause them to be of a greater spiritual nature. One would need to be extremely sensitive to be able to perceive the vibrations of this stone, for it is of a very delicate nature.

OTHER

In the future, jade will be used as a divining stone for an element that humanity is unaware of at this time. There are stones and rock formations in crystal form that are yet to be brought to light. These stones have been in the universe in times past, and will be discovered in some of the deeper caverns of the earth. They will be discovered in Burma, and be of a crystalline form and closely related to the rock crystal (as you perceive it). However, it will have another name and formation, and will be of great value, though not as valuable as the diamond.

Jade is the stone which many times causes man to be aware of his antiquity, of his own beginnings, of those things which are out of the past, because it represents many of the things which come from the orient, and again, represents the antiquity of the stages of man. Jade represents peace of being, depth of character, and an on-goingness, those which will last eternally.

This stone is also a guide to man, to be well aware of its smoothness and purity, of its satiny character. Man needs to be aware of the fact that his own image is imprinted on time, much as statues are carved of jade. There is a translucence about them/him, but it is not perceptible in the sense that one is able to see through himself or his fellow-man, but only that he can see the light of the Father reflected in the being of another person.

Jasper

Jasper is an opaque variety of chalcedony, commonly colored red, yellow, dark green and greyish blue, and is found in abundance the world over.

Noting that jasper was on the breast plates worn by the high priests, how would you define its qualities?

SPIRITUAL

Jasper is a stone of very subtle qualities. It does not give off strong vibrations, nor are the powers with it extremely strong. However, it is a stone that will work over a long period of time, one that has the ability to make long-term changes instead of sudden changes. It can be used in healing, but it is not something which can be placed over a particular hurt or wound. It is not of a vibration that affects the blood greatly, but it can be of a greater value if it is worn in or near the throat, and yet below the throat chakra, recognizing that it affects things as they come up to the head and face. It should be worn over the top of the breast bone. In this manner it subtly changes the vibrations from the lower part of the body (the area below the diaphragm) as they move up into the head.

Put a piece of jasper in water, and allow it to sit for two-three days, and then drink the water. This is the feeling of slow changes, putting it into the system, and yet not really into the blood stream. This sets the stage for other changes that will come. It readies the body to be able to receive other vibrations that could be of a more helpful nature. It is as an under-girding or strengthening character when imbibed into the system in this manner. It does not do the work in itself, but prepares the way for it. This can be considered as a general body tonic, and when used, it should be with the green jasper.

Do not expect miracles, as this is not a stone which will work in a rapid manner, nor does it perform great things, but because it does not, it is able to be more easily assimilated by all of the bodies that will partake of it. (The etheric, as well as the physical.) It is something that will not be rejected by the system; it is one of the areas that you do not need to worry about over-indulging or over-doing.

HEALING

Only as it causes the energies of the body to be subtly changed or slightly renewed or set in line, does this help to aid or abet healing. Jasper is not for a particular disease or problem, but only to get the vibrations of the body in a right direction, a balanced direction.

ENERGY

Jasper is able to emanate a slight radiation that is on the positive side. It is more useful when worn close to the body than at a distance, as it deflects the energy of the body back to it, only in a slightly changed form. Always changing, never the same, it has the ability to be used in a way that is supplemental to the body's own energies, rather than as an additive.

Jasper has the ability to correspond with the vibration of the opal, and could be used in conjunction with it, as it can both supplement or complement the opal, having the effect of tempering or balancing much of the fiery aspects of the opal. In essence, it causes a parallel energy to be in play along with that which the opal gives off, so that it would be of a less destructive force for the body, keeping the opal from being overly active.

It is well to use the jasper with those areas in or near the chest or at the lower throat area, as these are the areas where there is more congestion of blood and surface blood cells.

The beauty of each stone lies within the polishing. It can be a common ordinary stone, and yet when it is polished and turned into a fine piece of jewelry, it can be beauty in its simplicity. It is well for man to remember this and know that regardless of the adornment which goes on his body or in his mind, he must still recall the basic beauty and truth that is within him, namely that he is connected with the "All-Creator." His physical body is "earth;" close to the earth and very fundamental, while his mind and spirit are "at one" with the Creator, and he is, in essence, two beings simultaneously. This is essential for one to remember, for when he is looking at the basic stones, he should recall that he is as common as they are, and yet, when he looks at the beauty of a diamond, he should realize that he is able to be all things at all times, much as the many colors that reflect themselves within the diamond.

The areas, the colors, the hardness of man are as varied as the stones. Knowing these things, one must learn to turn within and think on his own goodness and qualities. Reflect on this.

Kunzite

Kunzite, a variety of spodumene, generally ranges in color from pale pink to deep lilac, and is phosphorescent under the influence of radium.

How would you describe the qualities of kunzite?

SPIRITUAL

Kunzite is a stone which causes a person to be more disciplined. It is essential that the wearer of this stone follow through on whatever particular task they are starting, for only as they follow through will they feel the benefit and the good that can come from the wearing of this particular stone. It has a rhythm about it, a regularity, a balance or rhythmic quality which causes the wearer to be more disciplined. Those who are erratic in their actions or in their emotions would find that this has a steadying influence for them. It is almost as if a force were causing them to be drawn into the path that they need to go. It is a gentle but forceful impact that this stone has upon the wearer.

HEALING

Kunzite could be considered healing only as it causes a freer flowing of the blood, as though it were "unblocked" or thinned. This is not something which causes the blood to *be* thin, but only causes the flowing of it to be more even in its course, or less viscous.

Kunzite is very helpful in working with tenseness in the shoulder. If it is held over the surface, or moved over the area of the shoulders, two-three inches away from the body, it has an effect of bombardment of the nerves in the shoulders, which eases and relaxes them.

ENERGY

The energy emanating from the stone is more like an underlying force, or that which would be considered "foundation" in nature. Kunzite is a strength and a quality, but it is not an activity. There is an under-girding strength which comes from this stone, having an action much like a strong magnet would. It has the ability to bend or to force, and yet not in a harsh manner.

Kunzite is a stone that works more on the extremities of the body or the flow of the blood in the veins. It is not essential or necessary to the body centers.

OTHER

It isn't necessary to wear kunzite. Use it by passing it over the veins in helping the blood to flow; also over the extremities, such as the hands and arms, more so than the legs or feet. Use the stone for poor circulation or at times when the blood needs to course more through the body in a cleansing manner. For example, if there were an infection in the legs, use the stone over the arms and it encourages the blood flow to flush out or wash away the poison. The stone should not be held over the infirmity itself, because of the power of drawing that it has. It would cause the blood to be drawn *to* that particular area, and perhaps increase the problem or congestion that might be present. By drawing the blood away, or causing it to course into other areas, it is able to get the free flow going so that it brings the healing qualities to the area of concern, in essence, drawing away or drawing off that which is necessary.

The kunzite is a stone which is rarely used, and is not one which causes one to be meditative nor philosophical in particular. It is one which is more grounded to the earth and is basic in its nature.

Lapis Lazuli

Lapis lazuli is a stone of a deep blue color in its purer textures, but often it is found intermixed with white calcite containing flecks of gold or pyrite in its matrix. A large amount of lapis lazuli is mined in Afghanistan and the Russian Urals, but deposits of the mineral are mined in numerous countries.

Occupying the eleventh position on the breast plate of the high priest, this stone should be of more than passing interest. How would you define its qualities?

SPIRITUAL

Lapis lazuli has the qualities of fineness, of high intensity, and yet etheric in quality. It is a stone which enables a wearer to tune his own etheric body to the particular vibration of that stone, and in so doing, it facilitates the opening of many of the chakra centers. For one that is contemplating the opening of his centers using this stone, it is wise that he do this only with love in his heart, comprehension in his mind and with wisdom in his soul, for as this is done, he will find that new avenues are open to that particular life. It should be done with caution and not in a manner of curiosity.

There is a refinement of all the thought-forms when working with this stone, and because of this, it can bring matters to mind much more clearly than they have been perceived in prior times.

A good method to attune a person's etheric body to the vibration of the lapis would be to place the stone on the crown chakra during meditation. You will find that its actions are subtle and yet they are of a vibration that will definitely enable the wearer to gain a greater insight into all things which pass his way.

As you visualize the stone, it is well to quiet the mind totally and let the eye take in the picture or the feeling of the stone and try to project yourself within it. Visually, in your mind's eye, diminish your own body to the point that you could enter the stone and feel it around you like a shroud or a shawl. Be content with your first attempts at this, and do not try to rush it. It is an esoteric truth that one needs to become one with a stone or a plant or a body before one can truly take on a part of that vibration and work with it. Do this with the mind's eye and not the heart center, and as you do, you will learn to blend with the stone. Each time try to go deeper and deeper within the stone. It is not necessary to think thoughts or ask questions, but only to try to move into the stone and become one with it. A polished stone would be best for this purpose; the smoothing or polishing of this stone is important, as there is less chance of energy impairment than would be present in a rough stone.

HEALING

If you wish to employ the lapis as a touchstone for healing, hold it in one hand while you are working with the other. Encompass it; enclose it. In this way, you can utilize the stone in a healing manner. To do this, concentrate upon the stone until you become as a focal point within it, projecting your mind and thought through it to the other being. It then causes all things to be purified and cleansed by the time it reaches the recipient.

ENERGY

Lapis lazuli has a fine quality, a high quality, much as an electrical energy charge. You have to reach to this energy vibration; it doesn't come to you.

The energy pattern can be visualized and better understood if you will consider the colors of the spectrum. The
reds, oranges and yellows are the warmer, high energy vibrations, and as you progress into the greens and blues, you are
reaching into the more etheric or spiritual vibrations. There is
a far greater depth, though not near the activity, when you
reach these higher vibrational planes.

Lapis has a correspondence to gold; not the metal, but the
gold that is within a person. As you can learn to become one
with this stone, then you will be able to place your own personality to one side, and use the lapis as a focal point in your
mind's eye, knowing that as you do this, you can reach more
clearly to another being without taking your own personality
or qualities with you. It is then that you can see a person
clearly for what they are, and appreciate those attributes that
they contain without any form of judgment on your part; any
form of seeing, any form of measurement, whether it is good
or bad. If there is a need within the person that you are able
to discern, it would be well to hold the words that contain
this need. In this regard, just hold the word or words in your
mind's eye. It isn't necessary, for example, to think, "this
person needs peace." Just hold the word "peace," and whatever is right, goes to that person or draws it forth from them.
With this stone, it is not for you to say, "Please bring this
person peace," or "Help them to find the right kind of life so
peace will come." You don't do any kind of aiding or abet-
ting, but merely hold the word or thought.

While many other stones can be employed as diviners for
metals and gem stones, it is a divining stone only for the
human body, divining the gold that is within the person.

OTHER

The lapis affects the kundalini center and also the heart
center. It can be used to raise the kundalini fire from its

repository, and causes that to be the goal which is sought; the divining of the liquid gold within the soul. Your mind becomes refined, much as the gold that has been through the smelter process; only that which is pure comes through and remains in the pure form.

Think on this, for this is the depth of learning that will need to be tapped in future days. We are coming into a New Age when all people will need to be aware of this kundalini force and be able to use it to their highest ability.

To use the lapis to influence the kundalini, it would be well to wear the stone(s) in such a way that it comes very close to the throat center or chakra which controls the will, being aware that the kundalini will always seek this higher center or "reach for this particular stone." It need not be thought on nor concentrated upon, but only worn. This technique is only for the person wearing the lapis, not for bringing the kundalini forth from another.

Although the lapis lazuli is popular as a ring stone, and was used by the prophets of old to "point the way" when worn on their right index finger, it is well to wear the stone oriented *above the diaphragm,* so that the energy is always being drawn up to the higher, spiritual centers. The same energies, when drawn "down" into the gonadic glands, can be of a "less positive" nature. The use of lapis in earrings, necklaces, chokers, broaches and other forms of jewelry worn high on the body, will best serve the wearer.

This stone needs to be considered as *one of the greatest,* although monetarily, it is deemed less valuable than many of your gem stones in popularity today. Lapis lazuli should be considered much as the center of the earth, the center of rotation, the center of centrifugal force; a focal point, much as the Sun relates to its solar system.

It has a great deal of energy or power, and yet it is only as good as that one who wears it; only as poor as that one who wears it, recognizing that of itself, it truly does not exude a great deal of power, and yet it is able to bring forth the power that is already there within a person. It enhances that which is, but does not "give" a great deal. It can be considered a leveling force, causing the energy and knowledge of that particular being to find its own level.

Malachite

Malachite is a stone ranging from light to dark green, often varigated and in uneven bands. It is one of the basic ores of copper, and is usually found in association with azurite.

Although malachite is basically an ore, it is often polished and used as decorative jewelry and carving. Is there much of value to this stone?

Malachite is variable in its condition. There are times when it is of a very positive nature, and also times when it is of a negative nature. It reaches to the inner part of man and reflects that which is already within him, and consequently when he *feels* this stone as a negative thing, it is only because it is reflecting his own negative qualities. It might be said that this stone could become the mirror of the soul, for through it man can see himself more clearly than his neighbor. Be open and candid with yourself when considering this; there are times when we are not able to look at that which we would see, and because of this, not realize that the negativity is of one's own making. It is well to analyze this carefully, to reflect on it and use it for your growth.

Because malachite is variable in its condition, caution must be exercised in wearing it as jewelry. Always reflect on how you feel at the time of wearing the stone, and if you are feeling in a negative mood, do not wear it. When you feel your "mood swing" is on the upward trend, malachite amplifies that mood, and would be comfortable to wear.

HEALING

There is a slight change upon the etheric body with this particular stone. It does not affect the physical body, but it does affect those areas which in turn have an effect on the physical body. It is of a finer quality, and something which you could not see with the naked eye, but be assured that it has the ability to attest to the truth that is within a person. Malachite is not of great value, but it can be used on an inner level.

ENERGY

Malachite is able to correspond to the para-thyroid glands; however, it does not influence them, nor should you try to work with them using this particular stone. Only know that even as they are in two parts and affect each other, so does this stone affect the sides of personality of man in the same manner. Malachite is not to be used in a manner of healing, nor of drawing energy forth, nor of putting energy in, but recognize that its energy pattern corresponds to this particular part of the human body. *Never* attempt to use this stone in healing, as it is not always of a safe nature, inasmuch as when you are working with a segment of the person, you are not sure what their particular temperament is at that time, nor what their cycle might be, and you could well be amplifying that which is negative within them. Always allow the will of the person to be the directing force.

If malachite amplifies the positive and negative qualities,

are you saying that the para-thyroid glands have something to do with the cycle of the emotional and mental bodies in their relation to the physical?

The para-thyroid glands have the power to give or withhold energies from a person. They are that which causes the balance and the flow to be within the body. They are that which can energize the body and which can also deplete the body of its energy.

Orange jade would be of benefit in the area of the para-thyroid glands if a person were low in energy, as it has the soothing energizing qualities of an amount that these particular glands could work with. However, *be cautious* in trying to stimulate these glands. Allow the stimulation to come from other areas of the body, using the glands as a secondary action in the energy flow.

When a person is hyper-active, it is many times due to the mineral imbalance within the body that is causing it. You will find that this is usually because of an excess intake of manganese through vegetables, for example, and yet it can often be because certain bodies allow this mineral to be filtered through their system more rapidly than others. It is caused more by the inner workings of the body than the area in which you live. One of the best ways to remove this excess of manganese is through the use of cell-salts.

OTHER

The wearing of malachite is *not* always the wisest choice. If it is worn, it should be worn as a ring, and taken off when it is deemed necessary. It should be something that is easily removable, and not worn close to any particular organ. If it is worn on the ring finger of the left hand it is not harmful. If so, it should be highly polished.

It is well for man to be aware of his own dual nature, knowing that many times those things which come to him that are of a lesser quality, he enhances by his own thought-forms which abound with him; and likewise, those things which would also appear as good luck or good fortune he can enhance and cause them to be even greater.

Many times he is aware that he is the changing point or the balancing effort with that which comes to him. He need not work dramatically with this, but only understand that *through him* do all things become that which they are. *He* is the creator; *he* is the one who adjusts the thought-form to become an actuality or a reality, and through this does it become good or bad, great or small.

Moonstone

The moonstone, a variety of feldspar, and more correctly called orthoclase, is generally of a milky, bluish opalescence and is of interest to the eye because of the sheen that is reflected from the stone.

Is there anything of value, of an esoteric nature, in the moonstone?

To those who are of a negative nature, it is a very negative stone, while to those who are of a positive nature, it is also a very positive stone. It incorporates a person's being and feelings, yet it does not add to nor detract from it. It is much as a mirror or a reflection of the one who wears it.

Moonstone is excellent for psychometry and for pulling together the inner self of the person, for through the moonstone the being is reflected. Note: The esoteric description of psychometry is "The Law of Association of Ideas applied to the vibratory quality of force for the purpose of obtaining information."

As used in psychometry, those who are able to read the auras of other people through the use of a particular metal or stone, will find that this is the stone which gives the true character of the person being "read." It does not hide the inner personality, but gives in truth that which is with the wearer. It draws vibrations from all the levels of "being," and yet only in minute quantities. It does not draw off the negative, it does not add to the positive, but gives a truer picture of that which is there. On a very subtle level, it perceives that which *is,* and is able to divine it in such terms that it is made clear to the one who is seeking. It can be very truthful, and yet give each of the interactions of the emotions, one with another, so that the total picture can be made quite clear.

To do this effectively, the stone should belong to the wearer, so that the one who does the psychometry is then able to pick up the total life pattern, for there are minute particles with this stone that tell all that has been and will be, all that is there. It is not of value for the psychometrist to own, but only to use when brought by others. The moonstone picks up the vibrations of the wearer; their total picture, past, present and future. For it to be effective in this manner, however, a person would have to wear it on their person for a minimum of three months. Any length of time would be helpful, but the longer, the better.

ENERGY

The solar plexus is antagonized by the moonstone, much as a grain of sand affects an oyster. It irritates the solar plexus, and yet it brings things into clearer focus. It helps a person to see themselves more clearly, to get the total picture.

This is not an aspect that man needs to develop in his own being, as there is nothing within the moonstone that would enhance his growth or even enhance his view of himself. He should consider it as an "outside energy" to be looked at, and yet, not take it into his own being.

There is nothing here that would be of a constructive nature for him, but only to consider that in life there are certain things which must be passed by which can be enjoyed for a short period, but are not necessarily part of the total life experience.

Onyx

Onyx is a variety of chalcedony, often characterized by black and white bands and popularly used in carving cameos in earlier times.

Is there anything of value to the onyx?

SPIRITUAL

This is a stone which appears to have no great depth. However, you will find that it is a stone which is able to listen well to the many things of man, and is an excellent stone to work with when one is trying to use psychometry, or endeavoring to define that which has come from another body. It also has the ability to transmute the vibrations of another person; transmuting, in that it is able to accept the vibration and transmute it before the seeker is influenced by it. Knowing that those things which come forth from the onyx cannot be of a negative nature as they reach the seeker, they are transmuted in such a manner that they will be given a greater importance.

The onyx carries vibrations with it, and can tell a tale. Listen well to the story of the onyx, but do not expect great spiritual properties with it. It is of a nature which "latches on" and holds. It is a secretive stone and one which is also deaf to negativity. It does not draw the negative forces to it as other stones will do; it mainly retains the story of the wearer.

It is similar to the moonstone in certain ways. Whereas the moonstone is one which will retain the spiritual qualities of man and the etheric body, the onyx is one which will retain the physical qualities and the physical story and happenings of man.

HEALING

Only as one needs a greater sense of physical strength or physical well-being, does this stone come forward. It is a stone which is like marrow to the bone or strength to the teeth. It causes a calling forth of the higher physical traits of man and causes them to be forceful within the body. It has the ability to call forth the fighting corpuscles which will bring strength to a body and fight an infection. The onyx can also be described as a plug that will not allow the body to be drained of any of its forces. It will help emotional stability during a time of battle, and could be worn daily as a strength-giving object. It has qualities that are very similar to sardonyx.

ENERGY

Onyx has an energy pattern that is stabilizing, neutralizing, strengthening. They have a great deal of value to one who might be easily upset, either emotionally or physically. This is a good stone for an athlete to wear, as the onyx brings balance to mind and body, and presence of mind. It brings the solid characteristics which are necessary to all of these professions, and it would keep them from being flighty of nature. Wear it on the left side of the body.

The onyx works well with either a pearl or diamond, as they both complement the onyx. When they are worn in combination, they are even more powerful. The pearl would bring about one effect, while the diamond would bring another. It is always desirable that the diamond or pearl complement this stone.

The onyx has a direct bearing on the solar plexus of the physical body, and also on the etheric body. It has the ability to cause the area of the solar plexus to be stabilized or less upset in its functioning or manner of operation. In this regard, it should be worn on a long chain so that it is down almost over the heart center when used by an athlete. Working through the solar plexus center, it stabilizes the pancreas. This area of the body can also be stabilized by using an onyx in a gold ring setting. An effective method would be to place the ring on a person's solar plexus while they are lying in a prone position during a time of meditation. Using this method, the ring would be removed from the finger.

The onyx is a stone which suggests that man needs to be of a solid character; of a strength within himself. He must be as solid as the stone is black; as bearable as the stone is in his reflective qualities, for even as the onyx can be polished to a high glaze, man must also be polished so that he can reflect the qualities around him, rather than mirror other people's qualities within himself. He must be able to reflect with joy, all those things which are around him. Give to others even as they pass, and in looking into the stone of this particular blackness, they will find their own beauty. Let this be their searching stone, and not their defining of another's qualities.

Opal

Opal is a stone of quasi-crystalline construction, formed ages ago through aqueous suspension. It ranges in color from a translucent white through all the colors of the spectrum, due to its refractive nature. It is generally classified as either common, black, precious or fire opal, and has long carried the superstition of being an unlucky stone.

How would you delineate the aspects of this stone?

Opal is a stone which can either diversify or scatter. Many who wear this stone are of a frivolous, frittering nature. The opal has the quality of amplifying a person's traits, so that if one is scattered or nervous in their thinking and actions, the opal magnifies this trait; if they are centered down in their actions and intent in their purpose, this is also magnified.

Wear the opal with caution! If you know yourself, if you know that you are not scattered, nervous, upset, then wear the opal, because it intensifies your ability to look into many subjects.

The stone is able to focus to the need of a person, although it is not of a strong vibration. For a general condition, it is able to go to the seat of a problem. The energy qualities are light, and yet they magnify whatever they come to, whether it be positive or negative.

One stone in particular, the fire opal, while good in working with business matters, can make the solar plexus nervous. Be receptive to this stone, and if you are feeling uncomfortable with it, remove it from your person.

In wearing the opal, it is best to wear it on your little finger, the farthest away from the body.

It would be well to keep the opal *away from teen-agers,* for at the time that they are most susceptible and open to the changing vibrations around them, this would cause them to be even more unstable. It is well that they look upon it but do not wear it, for even though it be their birth stone, it will not help to stabilize them. Until they have reached an age of maturity, between the ages of twenty-one and twenty-three, it is not the stone which would be the best for their use.

Pearl

While the pearl, like coral, develops from marine life and is not in a true sense a stone, it is worn or used in the same manner as gem stones.

Does the pearl have similar qualities that are akin to gem stones?

The pearl has its value in reaching to the "depth-of-personality." Even as a pearl grows through a constant rubbing together or irritating of a membrane, so a soul is also able to grow through irritation.

A pearl signifies purity and beauty, compassion and great love. This is in reference to the "perfect pearl," for there are so many that are slightly out of balance or "out-of-round." Even as this is true, so are many of the souls on the earth-plane not perfected. Those who are, are few, and yet they are able to let their light shine before their fellow man, so that it enables others to become more perfect.

A constant rubbing of a pearl between the fingers increases its luster and is excellent for use as a meditation piece, even as the luster of the human being will improve, as they are rubbed one with another.

The pearl can be used to focus the attention, and yet not to diffuse the energies of the body, as it is of an absorbative nature, rather than one which disperses energy.

HEALING

The pearl has no effect upon the physical body, but helps in the pulling together of the mental and spiritual forces; the culminating or combining of many areas of the body, and yet not of a physical nature. The pearl can be used to round out or soften the emotions and the intellect.

It also has the ability to respond to the pituitary gland, and is important in its soothing effect upon it. When there are great stresses put upon the body, it would be well to use this as a mounted piece, either in front of, or above, the pituitary gland.

ENERGY

Glowing, luminescent, peaceful, peace-bringing, are the qualities that are here. This would mean peace of mind and being, not peace to the body that is sickened with illness. The energy pattern of the pearl is just for the wearer. It cannot be transmitted to someone else. It has a quality of soothing and wholeness.

Would a cultured pearl be as effective as a natural pearl?

To a limited degree. Man needs to recognize that those things which are created without a natural need, are of a lesser vibratory rate. Those things which are created specifically for a purpose are limited in their outreach.

The pearl is insignificant insofar as being able to be used for the good of others. It is important that the one who wears or bears this particular stone, cultivate it and use it for their own benefit, recognizing that as they do this, they are able to centralize their thinking, their emotions and feelings, their thoughts and spirit into one particular area. It would be well to use this as an heirloom piece which is passed down through the family for many generations, as it will carry with it the continuing love and good vibrations of the past. It rejects all negativity and only holds the light or the positive.

The pearl gathers unto itself all of the love which is possessed by each of the owners, culminating in the final ownership of the particular pearl, and that one will be able to reap the benefits of the accumulated energy vibrations of love.

Peridot

Peridot, a light-green stone with a delicate tint, is a "first-cousin" to the olivine and chrysolite, and is often designated as such.

What are the various qualities of the peridot?

SPIRITUAL

It has the quality of lightness and beauty; the quality of seeing clearly and allowing problems to dissolve. Peridot is only for the very clear-minded person, one who is able to take the "long-view" of matters, and it would not be of particular help to those who are bogged down in life's problems, for they would be totally unable to grasp the quality or delicate vibration that is necessary to totally appreciate this stone. Its quality would be too light, too etheric.

HEALING

The healing qualities of the peridot are also very light. It is not for the healing of the body; it is for the healing of the spirit. It is for one who is troubled by the "discerning of spirit." It alleviates spiritual fear.

Peridot also causes the para-thyroid glands to be of a more balanced nature, giving them a lighter quality which is necessary for them to function properly.

This stone is only for those who are "very light," already in the spiritual realm. Those who are able to understand or have great sensitivity are able to use this stone for healing of their own spiritual uncertainty. The qualities here are extremely light, fine, not of a strong vibration. Even as this is so, the peridot serves as a protection against nervousness, which is a problem that needs to be worked with on the mental plane.

ENERGY

The energy qualities of the peridot are only perceived by those who are extremely sensitive. To the average being they would not be received, so do not be greatly concerned with this. Those who desire or need this particular stone will sense its healing ability, and yet, it is so fragile that it would not be of use to the general public.

The peridot affects the top three chakra centers in the etheric body, and specifically, the crown center. If worn in a crown or in a headdress, this would be the most effective way to influence this center. It would be a soothing sensitivity, and yet it does not strongly affect this center. If used for this purpose, it should be worn in front of the center; otherwise it would be best to wear it at the base of the throat.

Ruby

The ruby is a variety of corundum, and its deep-red color has endeared it in the hearts of gem fanciers since earliest recorded history. One of the more scarce stones, it is found as a clear, deep-red color and frequently in a mottled reddish-purple color with the star stone.

What are the many aspects of this stone?

SPIRITUAL

Love is the quality that is reflected by the ruby; love is the need that can be filled by this particular stone. Those who lack in self-love would do well to meditate on a stone of this color, of this quality. By so doing, they can release within themselves the energy that is necessary to overcome much of the trauma engendered by their lack of self-love.

This stone also encompasses the quality of courage; not the courage of "going into battle," but the courage to be able to seek the truth at all times; courage to be able to stand up for that which is right; courage to be the true part of one's own highest potential. Courage is a very commendable trait with this stone. It also could be termed valor.

HEALING

The ruby works well with the flow of blood, not as a blood purifier, but as an aid to the circulation and free flow of the blood. It aids in the cleansing and removal of infection or germs within the blood-stream, and in this manner can be considered a purifier.

The ruby can also be an aid in working with blood clots when used in conjunction with a prism. The stroking of the ruby over the veins in the direction of the heart can be a very helpful action when there are blood clots present. This must be done cautiously and without irritation or fear, for the work is delicate. In this case, the ruby would need to be faceted much as a "brilliant" cut diamond, and the point of the ruby would be used by the healer to go over the different main arteries or blood vessels. The prism could be placed on a table near by with a light playing through it, projecting the spectrum of colors within the room while the healer is using the ruby. It is not necessary that the light from the prism be played on the patient; the ruby is able to pick up the vibration and magnify it so that it can be used more on specific things such as clots or cholesterol. It is generally used for cleansing, however.

The adrenal glands, due to the purifying of the blood which has taken place, are stimulated and benefitted, as the adrenals are then better able to pick out each of the nutrients that they need from the blood and use it in its purer sense without having to wait for it to be clarified or purified through other organs first. It is a more direct process when purified by the ruby just before entering the adrenal glands.

The ruby is also excellent for use in stabilizing the eyes if it could be done over a period of years. It will not repair vision, but is helpful in maintaining that sight which you have. The increased blood flow caused by the ruby would help to reduce impairment to the eye. There is not a stone that is available to mankind at this time that will restore good vision.

The ruby affects the blood vessels that are in or near the eye and causes them to be able to maintain or strengthen themselves so that they can stay at that particular stage in time. The stone strengthens the infinitesimal or minute walls or cells and helps them to hold their present condition.

There are other aids that would be effective in restoring good vision, but there are no perfect answers as yet, for man has not yet learned to take care of that which is his to endure. He must learn to take care of each part of his body as though it were the only part, and yet man feels that he doesn't have time for each of these areas. This would be a total response; the need for proper nutrition, proper care, proper lighting, proper "many things," and man has not yet been able to see himself as a total picture, but only as a series of parts.

ENERGY

The ruby has a cleansing effect on the centers which are most involved with the flow of blood in the body; more particularly, the heart center, the solar plexus center and the lower centers of the body. The emotional body is also easily affected by this stone, as it is of a very sensitive nature and can pick up the finer vibrations that the ruby is able to throw off.

In reference to the solar plexus, the ruby has a very disquieting effect upon it, as it causes much to be stirred, much to be brought forth, and is not one which soothes or quiets. This is not to imply that it is a destructive stone; it isn't. It is only drawing forth all of the energies in the proper way so that they are able to accomplish that which they are there for.

The ruby can be worn as a broach, as a ring to reflect upon or to look through, or even as an anklet. As an anklet, it keeps the stone away from the solar plexus, and can do its work at the vantage point of understanding of the body, inasmuch as all of the blood will at some time circulate through that particular area and receive the benefit of the ruby. It is not as disruptive when it is in this particular position, and if worn there, it should be on the inside of the leg, just forward of the ankle bone.

OTHER

There is an interesting relationship that the ruby has with a planetary body. There is a planet in space that has not yet been recognized by "modern man," and will not come into his focus until the close of the twentieth century. The planet is named Noele, which could generally be construed to mean, "Blessings from on high!"

When this planet is brought into the vision of man and into his understanding, he will then be able to deal more fully with the ruby and use it in the way in which it is intended to be used. This will be at a time when he is more spiritually able to cope with these matters. Noele is the fore-runner of the New Age, the planet of enlightenment.

The best of beauty and sparkle that is with this stone needs to be encompassed within mankind, for as he has the depth of love within his heart that can be reflected to all those whom he encounters, then will the world become a better place to reside in.

It is necessary for man to reflect upon each of these stones in their varying degrees, so that he will be able to look within himself and find these same qualities. The ruby is a patient, deep, moving stone, and one which has the hidden fires of courage and strength within, even as man must locate these qualities within himself.

The ruby is a stone that one should meditate upon, seeking for himself those qualities which are portrayed here. As he does this, he will find that he is exercising his own mind and his own strength, and thus increasing the qualities which are necessary within himself.

Sapphire

The sapphire, another variety of corundum and sister to the ruby, is a highly-prized gem, ranging in color from black, blue, white and gray, many times displaying a six-pointed star on its surface.

What are the many qualities that go with this stone?

HEALING

The sapphire is a stone which will bring lightness and joy, and yet depth of beauty and thought to the wearer. Those who wear this stone as a ring, are those who tend to work with healing of the mind or the spirit. It is well that those who wear the sapphire use it as a source of beauty around them, knowing that as they do, there are certain vibrations that emanate from this particular stone.

It is preferable to wear the sapphire as a ring, rather than as a heart stone. As a heart stone or pendant, it draws to the wearer a certain amount of *destructive force;* it draws other people's problems or troubles to them. As a ring, it sends out healing.

The blue stone is better for the qualities of healing. The black is better worn as a protection or as a stone which centers the wearer's body and forces. The white sapphire is of a high spiritual quality, and is an excellent stone to center one's attention upon, such as you would focus on a crystal. It is much as a focal point, a center of the mind.

There is also a slight difference in the use of a star sapphire in relation to a clear stone. The star sapphire is more effective in working with the chakra centers of the etheric body. The clear blue sapphire works more effectively with the mental body.

ENERGY

The sapphire centers or focusses energy without the conscious doing of the wearer. It emanates energy on its own, and is advisable for certain personalities to wear, more so than others. The sapphire has a vibration "all its own," working independently, rather than just adding or supplementing the energy of the wearer.

Sapphire is most effective when set in pure silver, as silver doesn't detract from the vibrations of the stone. This is not to say that sapphire has a correspondence to silver, but only that they blend or go well together.

Is there a particular symbology to the star within the sapphire?

As you concentrate upon the star or gaze into it, you are able to center your thoughts, to focus your own being. It is a constant reminder that all things go out from the center; that one must reach in many ways to become whole. It is also showing you the elusive quality of truth or good, for even though you gaze at an object, you cannot see its true beauty until you see it under the strong, bright light of spirituality. As you gaze at it from one point, you are able to see the beauty within it, and yet if you care to rationalize it, or work it to your own feelings, you are able to make it appear off-center.

Even as there are many paths to follow on earth, so are they always and ever crossing each other, as in the star sapphire. Regardless of where a man begins his search, he will find that there is a focal point in the middle that he must reach, the focal point being the God-source, the God-energy. Even as he begins to reach to others who are also seeking, he will also find that they have a different starting point within the circle. Even with those things which would appear to be plain as the sapphire, plain as the colorles sapphire even, there is still the beauty and depth within, and man must look for these things in all of his goings and comings.

Sardonyx

Sardonyx is a stone distinguished by its red and white bands, and is one of the many varieties of chalcedony. It was the stone worn on the "breastplate" that was designated as onyx.

What are the qualities of sardonyx?

The desire to fight, to defend; physical combat! The paramount quality with this stone is of a defensive nature; the qualities which desire to defend or to seek out the causes to work with on the earth plane. It is a very physical stone, and is more given over to those of aggressive temperaments or dispositions; those who are the explorers, those in combat.

HEALING

Sardonyx has an effect upon the bone marrow, or that which is deep within the bone, and can help to alleviate cell disturbances within the marrow. When properly blessed and *focussed,* sardonyx is of great benefit in treatment of cancer of the bone marrow, however it would also require the conscious acceptance on the part of the one to be healed.

The employment of this stone in this manner is not available at the present time. Do not feel badly about this, but be assured that in the years to come there shall be the opening of this information to the medical world. Just recognize at this time that this can be one of the purposes of the sardonyx, employing high frequency laser or x-ray beams, with the energy of the beam being projected through the sardonyx.

Man must learn to differentiate the varying parts of his life and his existence so that there is a time for work and a time for play; a time for health and a time for sickness; a time for all things, even as this stone has been able to separate the bone and the marrow, knowing that there is a specific purpose for everything.

Tiger's-eye

Tiger's-eye is actually the more modern term for the mineral, crocidolite, which in its more common color of golden-brown, is the oxidation of the original blue hue. It is another variety of chalcedony which has replaced deposits of asbestos ages ago.

Is there anything of value in this stone?

Never judge a stone by its material worth! This stone is ever-changing within itself, much as it would appear to change to the observer when viewed from different angles. This stone becomes to the "mind's-eye" as an "all-seeing" eye, and this is important, for as one is able to wear this particular stone and focus upon it, it gives them the feeling of oneness. It causes that one to feel more strength, more direct, more pointed in their belief and their thoughts; more totally channeled and challenged in their way of being.

This stone causes a focussing of the mind and the *power* of the mind. This is an important stone, *but only for those who will use it rightly!* By this is meant being aware of one's own needs, and the needs of others, for through this one can then see that there are many different points of view, many different areas, many different planes of growth. It is necessary to be able to relate to your fellow human being in such a way that you can understand their weaknesses and their strengths. It is necessary that you learn that even within *self* there are weaknesses and strengths, and it is not necessary to feel less than good because there are these areas.

This stone can be used mainly for gazing upon, reflecting upon, and by using its satiny surface as a thought-soother.

HEALING

The tiger-eye does not bring strength to the body, but more importantly, it brings strength to the mind and a centering of the thoughts. It is much as a "direct pole" to center around; a thought-form which can be created within the mind and forced out into the ethers to bring about that which needs to be; not those things which are intangible or wishful in their manner or thinking, but those things which need to be for that soul's good. This is the direct power of the mind and to the mind.

Do not anticipate any bodily healings with this stone; it is more on the material plane that this can be used, and even so, it will be used to greatly increase the psychic ability and power of that one who wears it and *uses it properly,* as well as their ability to understand that which they are working with.

It will bring about those things on the material plane that are necessary for that particular soul's good, or to draw to him those other souls that are necessary to him. This may be considered in your mind as the physical plane, and yet it is considered "material" in our eyesight.

ENERGY

There is a pulsating energy with this stone; reaching out and drawing back; however, the *drawing back* is never of a negative nature. It continues to pulsate and cause a rhythm. This particular rhythm is that which helps to vibrate that particular soul to, and with, the Universe, much as a metronome. This should not be confused with "energizing," however, as it is not a stone which will add to the energy, but only to bring those things into balance which are necessary.

"Continually seeking," could be another term for the vibratory expression of the tiger-eye; continually reaching out, continually finding that which is necessary to be found. This stone can be termed an activating stone. It is good and positive, but strict and stern in its outreach; important to the mind, causing the mind to be activated, centered and powerful.

The tiger-eye should be worn in a wide bracelet with an oval-shaped stone in the middle, and worn on the right arm. The bracelet should be made of either silver or copper, silver being preferable. It can also be worn as a ring.

As you think on this stone, remember that man must ever be pliable and open; he must constantly be looking to those things around himself, that he might learn the lessons of the earth, for as he looks upon this stone, he will see that as he varies from one side to another, the hues and the tones can change. This is necessary for him to be aware of, for even as he looks at his fellow-man, he will see that the moods change; that time swings from dawn to dark, from right to wrong, from good to bad, from positive to negative. It is well that he learn to seek and watch this and approach his fellow-man only when the timing is right, or when the color is there. It is well to be perceptive and aware of his fellow-man's needs, and change with these as is necessary.

Topaz

Topaz is generally golden-yellow in color, but it can range from colorless to pale blue, pink and brown. Although topaz is not prized as highly as diamond, ruby or sapphire, from the point of view of occult symbolism, it ranks extremely high in the hierarchy of precious stones.

How would you classify the topaz?

This gem has rather interesting qualities. It is less demanding than the diamond on the consciousness, as it does not cause one to reflect against the extremely pure, clear qualities that a diamond reflects, and thus the personality is able to be softened by the yellow glow of the topaz.

SPIRITUAL

Topaz has the quality of light, of joy, of love within its vibrations. This is a gift of love from the giver to the receiver. It is a delicate stone, and yet it has great strength within it. The light within the topaz is easily transmitted from one to another, and even when it is dulled or marred, it continues to send out its light radiation of a delicate quality.

Topaz is also a stone of expansiveness; that which gives out or gives forth, and this is one of the important qualities of this stone. Always keep this aspect of the topaz in mind!

Within the topaz are all of the spiritual potentials for mankind, for man is able to look into this stone or to feel it and be able to glow with it, knowing that the light and etheric qualities that are with it can also be a part of his own being. It helps also to radiate a spiritual love from man to all of his surroundings. It is a part of his own "giving-force" on the earthplane. He is able to rejoice with this stone, rather than to be condemned by it or to feel threatened by it. It is a loving stone.

HEALING

The vibration of the topaz creates a lightness of spirit, stimulating the feeling of joy, the beginnings of hope. It causes man to compare himself to his Creator, and even as he does this, he realizes that he is compared more to the softer qualities of the topaz than the hardened qualities of the diamond. Man is not expected to be pure and in all ways perfect. One can see the radiation of the golden light and know that because of this, it is like the sunrise; there is hope, there is a new beginning, there is a dawning. It is also like the soft haze of evening, for it causes a glow to be around him, transmuting those things which would appear to be too harsh, into the softer, more subtle qualities that are the human side of man. It is more symbolic in this sense than it is actual, for man does not think these things through, but they do reach his inner consciousness or his whole being, and this is the important level to be reached.

The golden light of the topaz is beneficial to the clearing of the consciousness. It causes the cells within the head to be released or relaxed, and causes the tension to flow freely away. This is in reference to the "tension" headaches that are caused by man through his own thinking and tenseness, rather than the headaches of actual physical disease, but the headaches in which the blood cells are constricted or restricted through one's own tightness of nerves and feeling.

ENERGY

Within the vibration of the topaz there is much benefit to the wearer. There is the constant reminder and lightness of being with it that causes the wearer to open to others. It also acts as a protection against depression and also insomnia. The main cause of insomnia is the troubled mind which refuses to be put at rest, and the topaz is able to absorb the lesser vibrations of the person and disperse them, absorb them, dissolve them; not to send them out into the ethers.

The most beneficial way to employ this information would be to wear it as a ring, and when lying down at night, to place your arm with the ring on it, near the forehead or third eye center. This will place the stone nearer to the source of the problem, and draw off the particular vibrations that are causing insomnia. The ring should be made in such a way that the topaz stands out from the setting, without being encompassed by many other stones. It should stand alone and work simply in that manner. It is always well when using a stone in this manner to later have it cleansed or blessed.

The topaz is most effective on the head centers (third eye and crown) because this is the area where many of the troubles of man stem from. However, it is effective and beneficial with all of the centers, as it draws off the negativity from the centers over which it is passed. It also draws off this negativity through the bloodstream flowing in close proximity to the centers.

The topaz, when held over any of the chakra centers, adds lightness and joy to that center.

You indicate that the third eye and crown chakra are the source of many troubles. What is implied by this?

Man has hardened his own being, his own way of thinking, his own thoughts, and this is the reason that he causes many of his own problems, for through his lack of being able to listen, to learn or to expand, he closes off many of his own opportunities. It is through this particular attitude that he brings many illnesses upon himself, for even as he tells other people that he is able to stand all things, as an example, within he is quaking with the prospect of having to stand these particular things. Man is his own worst enemy and this needs to be dispelled. The pineal and pituitary glands are two of the areas in which the hardening of thought is most readily perceived, for as man closes his mind or his thinking, so these areas also close down and appear to be incased in a shell. As the topaz is played upon these, they are able to open, to relax, to let the constriction or restriction move away and cause an opening of all of his being, so that he can expand and think into new areas or new ways.

In selecting a topaz, the yellow topaz, in its simplicity, is the one you should strive to find. Use it in the manner described above, recognizing that the other colors of topaz, such as pink and violet, do add some qualities, but they are not as "total" or "all-around" in their aspects. The citrine, while similar in appearance to the topaz, is formed closer to the earth's crust, and is of a very weak quality. This stone *should not* be confused with topaz.

The topaz can be worn most effectively as a ring on the left hand, and also as a pendant hanging over the thymus gland (heart center.)

The mind of man needs to begin to glow much as the topaz does, with the clarity and the gold that is there, the gold reflecting that which is Christ-like within himself, knowing that as he does this, he will be far more tolerant and understanding of his fellow-man. If he can be more muted in his thinking and in his actions than he would be were he to reflect the diamond qualities, he would find that he could be far more compatible with his fellow-man, and also understanding of the nature of the workings of the mind.

The topaz is mellow, and man must mellow in his feelings and his thinking, and his attitude towards all of nature, in order to be more translucent in his being.

Tourmaline

Tourmaline generally grows in hexagonal, prismatic crystals, and has one of the most complicated compositions of any gem stone, ranging in color from an opaque black through the complete color range of clear stones.

Would a stone of such complicated composition be of much value?

The tourmaline has varying uses, even as it has varying colors. Variation is a part of the quality of this stone, for it causes you to be more flexible, more understanding, less emotionally involved in your feelings with others, and yet more objective in purpose and reason.

HEALING

Tourmaline causes a reaction in the intestinal tract. The use of this stone should be over the solar plexus center, but *with great caution,* as it can cause a looseness, or what would appear to be a diarrhetic condition. *Tourmaline is NOT to be used lightly nor in inept hands!* It causes vibrations to be raised and lowered; emotions to be stirred and smoothed. Tourmaline is quite variable and can be used in many ways, and consequently it is difficult to give the exact usage of this, for it is such an individual thing that you would find that each person has their own need, and it would be best for each one to do their own receiving in the use of this particular stone, or to have the information channelled at the time that the need was there, because the directions of use would be totally different. This is because each person has a different response to this stone, and the stone, in itself, has a wide variety of uses.

Basically, tourmaline would be used for the intestinal tracts. It could cause, as we said, a rather diarrhetic condition; it could be a cleansing thing; it could be an almost constipating thing. It has the ability to cause an obstruction in the intestinal lining to be loosened or dislodged. For a person sensitive in the use of this stone, it would best be employed much as a crayon, tracing the tourmaline over the intestinal tract, where the vibrations of the stone will be absorbed through the body and into the tract.

ENERGY

The color of the stone has a relationship to the energy vibration, with black at the low end of the scale. If any of the stones were to cause constipation, it would be the black tourmaline that would cause it. Higher on the scale is the green stone, which causes a churning effect. Yellow tourmaline, which causes a smooth flowing effect, is close to the top of the scale, while blue and bluish-purple would be at the top. This latter stone would work best with organs higher in the body, such as the liver or kidneys.

The lydic center is influenced by the tourmaline, and can be stimulated by its vibrations; however, this must be used with great caution, as the stimulation should be of a *very minor* amount. It would be preferable to use the blue stone, in this case, as the yellow tourmaline would be too stimulating.

Note: The lydic center controls the spleen in the physical body, the area of inflow of much of the body's energy. Experimenting with this stone is definitely to be discouraged. Much useful informatoin has been deliberately withheld by the teachers, knowing that there will always be those who would attempt to try certain experiments on another's body, and this could lead to problems.

The tourmaline, whatever its color, should *not* be worn on the body.

The natures of man are as different as the colors within this stone. Man must contemplate this himself, and even as he does, he will recognize himself among the many hues and colors of the tourmaline. He will find that there are times when he is of a blocking nature; one which would stop much of the flow of his love from going from himself to others in the world around him. He would also find that there are times that he is much as the open flow of a loving and giving nature.

There are many times when he desires to help or heal his fellow-man; there are many times when he would be giving and loving, and yet, all of these things change, even as his mood and disposition change, much like the changing tourmaline.

Turquoise

Of all the opaque stones, turquoise stands alone as a prominent item of jewelry, and is fast approaching the ranks of precious stones. Ranging in color from sky-blue to apple-green, it is generally mined in arid, desert regions of the world.

How would you classify the turquoise, so long revered by the American Indian?

The turquoise stones are very meaningful, particularly to the one who wears them, for they take on the characteristics of the owner; they become the high and the low, the good and the bad, the right and the wrong for that particular person.

As one is able to acquire and identify with their own turquoise, they will be able to pick up the higher qualities, especially if they have become attuned to the more positive aspects of life.

SPIRITUAL

The turquoise is a stone that carries great wisdom with it; one which has a long history of greatness and glory, even though it is not of an expensive nature. The wisdom is not truly within the stone, but it does cause those who have the wisdom to appreciate it, to come forth with their own understanding, and this stone then enhances that which they will say, think or do. It is enhanced by the wearer or the one who is able to perceive its depth. You will find that only those who wear the turquoise with regal qualities are those who have the true understanding of nature and all that is upon the earth, for they are the ones who will seek out answers; they are the ones who will seek for the basic truth; those that you can require much of and they will be able to come forth and follow through with the answers and the wisdom that is necessary to help you in times of need. This may not appear to be true, for turquoise is one of the stones which is being worn greatly today, and there are those who wear it strictly for decorative purposes; however, know that even though they wear it lightly, or because they appreciate the appeal that it has, there is a wisdom that will come to them when they wear it long enough. The silver which is usually added to it is also of a beneficial nature to the wearer. It causes their blood stream to be able to pick up the vibration and carry it through to other parts of their body. Bless the use and wearing of this stone!

The turquoise is one of the stones of greatest antiquity; it is one of the stones which has been appreciated and fondled more than any other; a stone which has been worn with great pride and has had meaning to the wearer through times past. It is a stone which has been carved and petted and rubbed and polished and is of a very close nature to the one who wears it. Though of a lesser value than many other stones, there is a closeness between the wearer and the stone, as compared to stones of higher material value, whose owners place them in vaults and tend to "stand apart from them."

HEALING

The healing qualities of the turquoise are reserved mainly for the wearer, for as they are able to attune to it, it will be useful as a general healing stone; one for all illnesses, especially those of the mental body. However, this is only to those who are already gifted with healing. For others, it will be a meaningless stone as far as healing goes.

To best be employed as a healing stone, turquoise should be set in silver in a large bracelet and worn on the left wrist. This enhances the healing abilities when working in that manner.

ENERGY

The energy pattern is of great strength, of vitality, of steady, ongoing power. It works on the physical body, steadying, neutralizing and balancing the vibrations of the one who is wearing it.

It is essential that those who wear the turquoise be of a peaceful nature, for only as one is peaceful are they able to truly vibrate to it. This is a vital, energetic stone of great depth.

The stone need not be of the highest quality to be good for a particular wearer. Those who are able to identify with the stone itself, are best suited to wear it. As you check the different stones or have the feeling for one, it is best to buy that particular stone, regardless of where it is found. Even the poorer quality turquoise is good if you vibrate to it.

With this stone there is also a great sense of balance. Through the use of it, and the meditation upon it, one can find that life itself begins to come into a meaningful, purposeful place. The stone is not totally responsible for this, but it is the vibration of it which causes man to be able to react in a different way to the circumstances in his life. As he does this, he will find that people, in turn, react differently to him. This would be on a very subtle level, and the change could be noted over a long period of time.

The turquoise affects the glands through the will center in the throat. As you hold it to the will center, its energy travels to all parts of the body through the various glands and into the blood. It is not necessary to wear the stone over the throat.

The need for this stone to be in use is evident in the world today. It would be well if all were able to attune themselves to a piece of turquoise, and find the peace that goes with it. For those who are able to carve or work in jewelry, it would be well to model or work with it, for through it they will acquire great learning values. There are lessons to be learned in working with jewels and metals, and turquoise is one of the basics. It teaches to carve, it teaches to feel for where it should go; it teaches the one who is doing the work to mold that which should come forth.

This stone can be employed in many ways. It can be made into objects of beauty to be set in rooms that will be enhanced by their presence. It has a steadying influence upon the room; it is helpful to the one who wears it, but it is also well to have some on display where all may look at it and project love towards it and have it reflect back to them.

Zircon

The zircon is the "poor man's diamond," a species that deserves greater recognition than it receives. It ranges in color from red, brown and yellow, on into green and light blue; the clear color used in jewelry being derived by applying heat to the yellow and brown stones.

Does the zircon have any beneficial qualities to it?

Zircon is a quiet stone that causes man to be more at peace within himself. It causes him to reflect and direct his own processes of thinking; it is a peaceful stone. Its qualities would be considered lightness, peace, blending, peacemaker; a stone of harmony.

HEALING

The zircon is an aid in the healing of the spirit. Peace and spiritual temperance that are valuable, but nothing visible to the physical eye. The stone has a soft, blending quality to it, but it is not considered a dominant stone.

Those of a fiery nature would not be able to relate to this stone; only those who are already of a quiet nature will find the beauty and depth that is here, and they will be able to use this for the peace of their own mind, for through this stone they will be able to relate, not only to themselves, but to others around them.

ENERGY

Zircon is helpful to the breathing in the lungs. If it were in a large enough stone so that light could flow through it, the light would be helpful in keeping down congestion in the lungs. Not with emphysema, but more with polio or tuberculosis.

This could be of use with an iron lung, by placing two or three fairly large stones within the iron lung so that outer light of the Universe could be transmitted through the stones onto the bare chest of the person within the lung. It would cause their breathing to be easier. It would not totally relieve the condition, but it would greatly improve their response to the machine.

The best place to wear a zircon, if a large stone, would be as a lavalier over the chest area. In a smaller stone, as a ring on any finger.

The zircon will remind man that there are other things to life than just that which he sees and feels and is consciously aware of. He needs to learn that there are the higher, ethereal qualities about himself, even as there are within the stones. He needs to learn to listen for the quiet and the softness that is within his own being. This is difficult for him to learn, as many times he is so pounded and embattled by the sounds of the world around him that he is unable to hear the "still, small voice within." The zircon is of a lighter quality, that would remind man to *listen!*

Miscellaneous Stones

The stones on the pages following are in the miscellaneous classification for several reasons. In some cases, the energy patterns were of an insignificant nature; in others, they were not directly involved with the human kingdom, and in still others, their use for mankind is still far into the future, and consequently of an irrelevant nature at this time.

Relevant comments are included for their usefulness, or in some cases, for their future potential. Don't neglect to read them; what is "miscellaneous" to one, may be quite meaningful to another.

CITRINE

Let the buyer be wary that he not be fooled into thinking the citrine is the more valuable topaz. Citrine will not be of great benefit to him, and he needs to be aware of which stone he has.

CHRYSOLITE

The qualities of this stone are parallel to those of peridot and olivine, the difference being imperceptible. The information given on the peridot would apply equally to chrysolite.

FLUORITE

Fluorite has an effervescence to it that can be used in conjunction with other stones; it opens the way, plows the ground, softens the way for the use of other stones. As an example, if you were working on problem areas in the vicinity of a person's solar plexus, placing a fluorite stone in the area of treatment for about fifteen minutes prior to using another stone has the effect of softening the area or loosening things up. It is particularly good when used in this manner with any of the purple or yellow stones, such as sapphire, topaz, yellow jade or amethyst.

It would be well for mankind to know that fluorite imparts a necessary mineral to the water that is important for fish and for their growth. It adds to their ability to form bone, and it helps them to see better. This is especially true for tropical fish in aquariums. Merely dropping a piece of fluorite stone into the tank is beneficial to the fish.

Even as fluorite is able to open the way for other stones to be more useful, it is well for man to be aware of the influence of those with whom he associates. As he is close to certain influential, or less influential friends, they open the way for him to go to a greater or lesser path. We are all *one,* and a part of the One. It is necessary that all become *as* one, and work with a common goal or purpose, being aware that if we would choose the right, we must associate with it, and if we would choose the wrong, then we *do* automatically associate with it. Caution is necessary.

LAZULITE

Lazulite is similar to lapis lazuli, but does not have its depth of quality. There is a *sense* of healing with this stone but it is best used as a "worry stone;" a stone to be viewed or fingered.

The whiteness within it represents the purity in man, and the blue represents the spiritual qualities which need to be deeply ingrained, one with the other, for even as man is pure in his thinking, so he needs to be lifted to the higher planes of the realm, recalling that there is always a sense of purity within himself.

Many who are of a spiritual nature find that they are also able to increase or to incorporate greed and lust and many of the lower qualities of the human faculty with this particular spirituality, thus nullifying that good which comes through them or to them. Man needs to be far more aware of his own jealousy which creeps so often into spirituality. *Spiritual pride is one of the greatest of the evils that man is able to create within himself and around himself.*

PHENAKITE

Phenakite has the ability to disperse energy from other stones into many facets; it could be used as a disperser of the energies which come *through* it, and yet it can cause many stones to work together to work on many diseases or many problems at the same time. It brings the vibrations together and sends them out as one, drawing the qualities together and dispersing them as necessary. (Much as a medicinal pill with its various chemicals is held together until used or needed.)

It would take a great deal of technical knowledge to be able to use phenakite to its fullest extent. There will come a time in the future when it shall be more prevalent, and man shall then be able to develop his own uses for it. Know that it needs to be sought after and *stockpiled.*

RHODONITE

Rhodonite is beneficial when ground up into a powder and used as a medication. It protects the upper respiratory system. It has an effect upon the air passages within the lungs, aiding in their breathing capacity. It would take just a tiny pinch. Rhodonite would keep emphysema stirred to the point that it would not harden or dry into the cells. It is not a "cure-all" for this, but would help to keep it flexible, fluid. Rhodonite would be good for chemists to look into.

SERPENTINE

There will come a day when serpentine will be ground into a powder for use in machines and scientific research, but not as a commercial product; only as a material which aids and abets in the keeping of certain machines within their own *context*. It has its purpose and it will have its day; it has a potential within it that is not yet used.

SPINEL

Spinel has within its vibrations the quality or energy of causing one to try again, to have hope, or make another attempt.

It also has the ability to renew energy and vitality, but not on a long-term basis. It is sporadic in this manner.

Spinel works on the underside of both the solar plexus and the will center, bringing them into alignment with each other, causing them to begin to open if they are not already opened.

This stone should be worn quite low on the chest; about six inches down from the will center.

STAUROLITE

To each person, this stone has its own meaning. By placing it in front of the third eye chakra of the individual, they will be able to discern their own use of the stone.

The person who owns a staurolite must hold it in their hand and implant their own vibrations into it, and from that point on, they will find that it has a personal meaning and understanding for them.

To each, the cross has a different, inner meaning that is relevant and personal to them. Thus it can be used as a talisman, imparting the vibrations to the stone that the wearer would like to retain.

PRISM
(Man-made)

Although the prism is not a gem stone, it is made of silica, and in many cases, of quartz crystal. Due to its properties of bending light rays that produce the prismatic effect, it is projecting out energy vibrations over the entire spectrum of our vision, and can have an effect upon various stones.

In addition to this, much information of an interesting and historical nature came up as we probed for information on the prism; information we thought would be of great interest to many.

Mankind would do well to look into the uses of the prism more fully, as there is much to be learned from it.

The prism is of a nature which causes many changes, and brings about the total unfolding of that which comes into it. It is similar to a crystal in many ways, and yet it is not of the same nature. It would be well for man to learn to think of himself as a prism, and try to envision all of the changes which can come through him and to those around him, knowing that as their light comes to him, he is able to enhance it and cause it to become many beautiful rays, colors, or pictures, so that they, too, can see the unfoldment of the beauty that is within *them*. It would be well for each one to know how to enlighten his fellow man through this particular manner. He also needs to accept each of the words and thoughts that come to him from others, and know that as he receives them and adds his own thoughts and ideas to them, he is able to make them more manifold, more beautiful, more giving and loving, and as he does this, so they return to the sender, and from the sender they can again go out to another prism of man and become greater yet. This is the folding and unfolding, the multiplying of all of nature *within* man.

The prism is an effective device to use in a meditation group. With a beam of light projected through the prism, have the prism rotating slowly on its axis. As it rotates around the room, each person can think on any one of the spectral colors. Each color is integrated into a thought, and the thought is then projected to the body to be healed. Thus the colors are taken into the body, and each one is then able to work on the particular gland or organ that it corresponds to, and in this way, complete healing or wholeness can come. The prism is an excellent meditation object.

The main lesson of the prism is to show you that all can become one and clear, if they will but meld together in a balance with each other. It is the coming together or the oneness or allness of all things that *are*. This is only as an example, and yet it has clarity greater than even a diamond, for many times people stand in awe of the value of the diamond. The prism can be related to the common man, and he can see his place in the total picture of the universe, as he sees himself as one of these many lights which play upon the ceiling.

The prism is most effective in working with the mental and etheric bodies, and it should be recognized that as they are affected, so does the physical body become affected. None of the *bodies* of man are totally apart or separate from the others, and changes can come about in the others in a *reflec-*

tive way, just as having the light of the prism playing through the mental and etheric bodies.

You will also find that any of the gem stones used for a particular purpose can be enhanced through the use of the prism in conjunction with it. It would magnify the value of that stone, and it would also open the mental and etheric bodies for a greater function of the value of each of these stones. You do not need to hold the prism, think on it or through it, but only to keep it within the room.

It would be well to have a prism sitting in a room in such a manner that the sun could shine through it and throw its light into the room, even though one is not totally aware of it being there at all times.

In discussions on the "Lost continent of Atlantis," there are statements and reports of a type of prism that was used as a power station that provided a variety of energy for the area. Would you care to comment on that?

The prism of that time was used in a gigantic manner; it was used in such a way as to utilize the rays of the sun and the atmospheric conditions of the universe, so that they were brought into play on this planet. This energy was brought into this planet, broken up and re-arranged in such a way as to be used for power. It would draw this energy in and send it to a generator or a piece of machinery of comparable nature and store it. It was able to attract from outer space areas, the strong vibrations that are necessary to cause energy and power. When brought through the prism they were broken up into their respective forms and were able to re-arrange themselves into the forces that could be used by mankind. It was a force of Light and could direct outer beings to this particular area, as these beings knew where it was located and could be drawn in on its beam.

There is much to learn about the prism that mankind has forgotten. Dwell upon this and know that as the time is right and the need arises, many things will come forth that will validate the use and necessity of the prism.

Has this particular device been denied to humanity on the planet at this time because of its misuse at an earlier period in our history?

It has not yet been "re-discovered," nor re-used, but it is not being denied. It is only that man is not yet ready to spend his earth moments in the seeking in this particular manner. It will come in time. After the year 2000 A.D. it shall again be in use.

There will be those who will seek, and it will be given in bits and pieces, for there will need to be a cooperative effort from many sources before this can be given again. It is not denied, but it must be brought forth in pieces so that it will be a welding force, rather than a dividing force.

If many nations would work together on this, then the total picture could be brought forth, and it would then not be utilized by any one nation to the *detriment* of others, nor would it be given as an alleviation of problems to one, rather than given to all, for it *could* be so easily *denied.*

The prism that you referred to in your question, is presently in pieces. This prism has been broken through the centuries by the changing conditions of the earth; by the changing temperatures and climes and by the underground tremors that have caused it to be wedged in such a way that it has broken through the pressures of the earth.

It is presently located in the area that is referred to as Bimini Atoll. It could be found in pieces and in fairly large chunks, but it is not as one piece any longer. In its original form, it was a prism fifteen feet long, with an equilateral triangle of three-foot sides.

You should reflect upon the changeability of the prism, knowing that as man polishes his own surfaces, so will he be able to absorb the things which come into him and help to transmute them into even greater or higher things, causing them to be attitudes of beauty, rather than attitudes of negativity. Man should use this as a meditative object. It would be well to have one in every home.

The Metals and Ores

The ores and extracted metals might well be considered the "workhorse" of the mineral kingdom. There is little that you can scan in a normal day's passing that isn't involved with metal. A quick glance around a room can well show an amazing variety of metals that mankind has learned to develop for his use.

As in all things in nature, there is always the yin and the yang, the positive and negative, and this is true of the mineral kingdom. Minerals taken through vegetables, orally through vitamins and other methods are necessary and beneficial to our health and well-being, if not taken in over-abundance. Iron, steel and other metals form protection, comfort and safety; radium and uranium form a very needed function in medicine and metallurgy. These very same minerals, when used in weapons of destruction, can destroy civilization as we know it today. While it is an old esoteric truism that you cannot destroy "life,"—only the form, humanity has been given dominion over the three lower kingdoms in nature. It is our responsibility to use and develop these kingdoms in a proper manner, having a true regard for ecology and the proper employment or use of that which is available to us.

On the pages following there is much to point the way ahead to what may be attainable if we put our shoulder to the wheel and use the mineral kingdom for the betterment of mankind, rather than its destruction. No attempt was made to cover the many ores or metals that are available and in use today. We have considered only those metals which are common to jewelry, and a few others that were necessary to be brought to man's attention.

CINNABAR

Cinnabar is generally of a brick-red color, and is the principal ore of mercury.

What are the major qualities with cinnabar?

Cinnabar is an evaluator, and can be used in many ways to help determine or evaluate other areas of life. Mankind has already discovered this aspect of the ore in developing the mercury thermometer.

Cinnabar has energy qualities that are positive in nature, yet of a repelling nature. It is beneficial to physical forms, but nothing with "life" in it, such as humans, trees or plants can be benefitted by it. Objects and material such as cement, wood or stone, can. As an example, WHEN PAINTED ON A SURFACE, IT HAS THE ABILITY TO REPEL ATOMIC RADIATION OR BOMBARDMENT, and will be *extremely* beneficial and protective. This will become a valid fact in the years to come. You will find that it will be combined with other materials to form a shield or protective coating. When painted on cement or concrete, it will keep radiation out.

Cinnabar also has an effect upon the etheric body of a person, having a direct bearing on the solar plexus and heart chakras. It has a force field that causes them to be stimulated. Cinnabar (or mercury) is *not* something that you would use in a ring or in a piece of jewelry, but if held in a container over the solar plexus or heart centers, it would stimulate those areas of the body. This should not be used too often nor too directly, as it is a powerful force on these two areas, and consequently, any over-stimulation is just as bad as a lack of stimulation.

Cinnabar is one of the more common aspects of the earth, and yet it is necessary to observe the functions of the common sources and common things of the earth, that man might be able to relate to these, so he will see in his own commonness that he is as unusual as any of these other elements.

Recognize also, that abundance does not necessarily mean lack of value. Abundance only means that there are many needs and many things which one particular item can give or do. Because it is abundant upon the earthplane, there is a need or use that will come into being for it. Watch well, those things which appear in abundance.

COPPER

Copper is obtained from about seven different kinds of ore, and was one of the first metals used by early man.

What are the main attributes of copper?

As with other metals, it has the ability to attract to it those things which are within the body; the ability of drawing off the dregs of many things from the body, by oxidizing through the pores and eliminating some of the metallic wastes within. It can be helpful to some, but only as they have the need of this particular metal. Not all can benefit by its use, but when it is necessary, there is no other force on the earth that can remove those particular impurities from a body other than copper. Particularly with manganese, nothing else taken internally or externally could do the same job of removing that mineral from the body, should manganese be a problem. This is not to say that copper is the *only* method of removing manganese. The proper use of cell-salts can remove the mineral through the excretory system; copper removes it through the pores of the skin. Although manganese is a necessary mineral in the physical body, there are many bodies that are not able to handle more than a trace of this mineral, as they are not capable of throwing off the excess. It is then that copper becomes effective as a method of removing the excess.

By wearing a copper bracelet (clip-on type,) you can detect if your body has too much manganese in it. Underneath the bracelet there will be the sensation of burning, and if you experience this, you could then wear the copper bracelet for three or four days and then remove it for an equal period, continuing this process as long as you can detect the heat or burning sensation. Bathe the area with baking soda each time the bracelet is removed, so that it will neturalize those things which have come forth. Copper jewelry is not something that you should continue to wear for any lengthy time.

GALENA

Galena is a silvery-gray ore, and has long been used in radios with frequency control.

Are there any additional uses for this metal that have not as yet been discovered?

Galena is a metal of receptivity and of microscopic intensity. It is not used particularly for the health of the body nor of the being, but is excellent to be used in material ways. There will indeed be more uses of galena in the years to come, since each pore of it has a certain amount of receptivity, and it will be found that it can be used to trace back through time, and even forward through time, *when properly used.* Galena is an extremely receptive and sensitive metal.

It will be discovered in time to come, that galena can even

pick up the vibrations of the human brain and be used in such a way as to help transmit the thoughts of others. This is not something that needs to be played or tampered with in a negative or reckless manner, but when used properly, it will be of great help for those with mental disorders, as it will enable one to then discern their true thoughts or feelings. This will require the blending of three different types of metal in the wire that is connected to the galena. We refer to titanium, nickel and synopium. Synopium will be recognized as a combination of metals.

The above technique is not something that could be used over a long distance. There are minute particles of energy given off by galena that can be attuned to those working the set and to those near by, within the perimeter of a room. When perfected, the device will be able to find the wavelength of the person with the mental disorder, and be able to reach and broadcast the thoughts that are there. There would be nothing in the properties of galena that can send forth healing rays or vibrations, however. It may receive, hold and give off, but will not change the matter of that which comes.

Galena can also be effectively used as a divining rod for illnesses. Again, there will be a time ahead when man will develop this material to detect diseased areas within the body. Used much as a "geiger counter" or metal detector, it will employ a rod approximately two inches long and the circumference of a pencil that will be passed over a person's body. It will appear as a metal detector which would have sensitive wires within the rod that would be attached to the galena, and as it causes vibratory sounds to come through, you would be able to detect the perfection or imperfection of the body and know where the illness lies. There would be the need to establish comparisons in sound between healthy areas and diseased or unhealthy areas. The latter would have the sound of static from the receiver, in comparison to what will appear as the normal sound.

The uses of galena will be many, and it will take many years to perfect them. The glory of this stone is yet ahead.

Man must begin to equate himself with such parts of the earth as the gem stones and ores, for as he is able to study and dissect them, he will better be able to understand the total workings of his own mind and body. Man will have to realize that he is the same as the universe and all of the stars and planets; he is also the same as each part of the earth, and as he is able to define the impurities, the fallacies, the weaknesses and strengths of each of these things of the earth, he will see that he also contains these within his own being. Man has been wise enough to realize that his eye is like a camera and his brain is like a computer, but he needs to learn that these things were upon the earth long before any of the mechanical devices that are now within his own scope or range. These are only results of those things which were here before. He needs to realize that he is as receptive to thoughts and feelings as is this small stone, even as the plants are receptive to each person's thoughts and vibrations. He must also realize that even as he thinks and feels and does, so does he affect all of the particles and parts of the earth. He needs to be more totally aware of his actions, his thoughts and his own being; be aware also, that each of the cells of his own body are receptors or receivers of the many things which go on around him, whether they be of a positive *or* negative nature. He receives each of the vibratory rates of the world into his own being, and in this way he is much like the galena.

Galena is just another instance of the many things which appear to be lowly in nature, but are of the highest value to mankind, much as parts of the physical body which appear to be lowly in nature, many times perform the highest service. Even those areas of labor on the earth which would appear to be lowly are many times the most essential, such as those who serve the food of the earth, and those who work in the hospitals and do the simple and mundane chores.

These are the essentials, even though there are those who would do things that appear to be of a higher nature, such as the brain surgeon and other skilled professionals. It is only necessary to learn to put everything in its proper perspective. This is a part of the lesson of all of these stones; the perspective and the place where they belong in the "total picture" of the universe.

GOLD

Gold is one of the more dominant metals associated with gems and jewelry.

Is there a particular reason for this?

Gold is a metal of great value, for it is one which can be purified to a great extent. However, you must be aware that it always draws to itself great impurities, and thus it is that man is able to see himself reflected in this. As long as it is continually purified or put through the fire, it becomes even more valuable and thus can man relate to this, for as he is purified one time after another, he becomes more valuable in the kingdom of his own work.

Its particular aspects are that it can be worked with and molded and shaped, conformed to and with all other things. It is a metal which can be made into intricate or rough designs, and at all times it is capable of holding these things which it is given, namely stones. Recognize also, that when gold is in its purest form, it is the most fragile. Likewise with man; when he is in *his* purest form, he is most vulnerable to outside sources.

The metals are of a quality or porousness that causes vibrations to come to them, and consequently are prone to attract rather than disperse or give off vibrations. The stones and jewels characteristically energize, but the metals are those which draw forth or retain within themselves. Because of this, gold is used extensively with gem stones, because the metal is able to attract and hold unto itself those qualities which are given off, thereby providing a steadying influence for the jewels, for as they are able to emanate much of their own rate of vibration, the metal is then able to encompass or hold that for a steadying influence upon the body which it is to deal with. It many times can draw forth from the body some of the negative forces, while at the same time retaining the positive force of the stone, so that it acts as a balancing agent.

Gold is usually refined before it is of any value, and even as it comes in nuggets, it is not of a beauty to see. However, as it is polished and hammered and worked with, and as the lesser qualities are drawn forth from it, so does its beauty come forth. This is what man needs to ponder, for these are the things which he must do in his own life; to take away the dregs of his being, and cause the beauty to come forth with the polish of abrasion and kindness.

LODESTONE

Lodestone is a permanently magnetized stone that has been used down through the centuries as an amulet.

Is there an important implication to this stone?

The lodestone causes man to reach afar with his mind and send his thoughts into outer space, into outer realms, into the universal areas. Although the lodestone is not of great ability, it does have the ability to project out. It has the effect of causing man's mind to be released to some extent from his body, although it is not something that would be useful in astral travel or in that type of release from the body, but only in a mental way, projecting the mental body or condition to far places.

Lodestone also works on the lower part of the lungs, the lower part of the rib cage; it causes a warmth or energy, much as one might expect x-ray treatment to feel. It could be beneficial in the treatment of pneumonia-like conditions or lung congestion. It would not be greatly useful in emphysema, but it is beneficial to the lungs. It causes a certain amount of stimulation, much as a heated area might be stimulated.

Its effect with pneumonia is a subtle motion or action, one which causes the cells of the body to begin to respond and to do the jobs they should be doing. It does not cause a quick action, nor one which would be totally felt by the body, itself. To work with the lungs, two pieces of lodestone would be needed, one held on either side of the lungs and out in front approximately eight inches, projecting the energy over the lower ribs, allowing them just to be aimed at that area. This causes the blood vessels or cells to begin to churn, to come into action. Gradual stimulation has the effect of drawing the blood forward and back, so that it can cleanse itself and move on through the system. This method is excellent in treating tuberculosis also, if used daily in the manner described above. It doesn't show any visible effects, but it does begin to help.

Lodestone has an affinity to oil, and can be used as a divining stone in seeking out those areas of mineral wealth. However, it would be dormant as a divining stone except in the hands of one of high intentions. The technique or method will be given out at a time when man can recognize the harm he garners through material greed, and will use the information for the common weal.

SILVER

Silver is a metal quite popular in conjunction with jewelry, and has been used considerably as a medium of exchange around the world.

What are the main properties of silver that are important to know?

Silver is not as refined as gold, yet it does not need the constant working with it that gold does. It is pure in its own sense, and yet it is also able to attract many of the lesser vibrations to itself. (It has more of the physical qualities, where gold really attracts more of the spiritual or etheric qualities; being held in the gold and refined by the stone.)

Silver attracts the physical or lower qualities, the heavier things to itself, and at the same time, gold is usually considered more of the woman's material, while silver is considered the man's.

There is a strength with silver; there is also a staunch quality. It is less materialistic in value, and yet it is strong in its character.

Of all the metals, gold and silver should be considered of the greatest importance. These are the two metals that are destined to be a part of the past and a part of the future. You will find that they always return to man in one way or another.

Summary

With all of the material completed, there was the "one last question" to be asked: "Is there any additional information to be added, or final comments to be made before we wrap it up?" The answer was not too surprising: This book will cause controversy and dissension, but it will not be a great problem, for many things will come forth from it that will be beneficial to mankind. Do not be easily upset or disturbed by those things which come back as a negative report, but only know that much good shall come.

Any time new fields are plowed, new ground is broken, there will be those to contest what has been presented. This may appear to be negativity, but it isn't. Within our higher consciousness, our spiritual "Christ-self," there is the unity of all with the one God. Only as we express ourselves within the lower octaves of Light, do we take on aspects of consciousness that have a definite interplay with each other; aspects that when perfected, will be as one of the facets of the soul that has been mastered. It is this catalytic action between souls that creates growth, understanding and eventual attunement with each other.

What are these aspects? They are many and varied. As an illustrative example, we have portrayed within the New Testament of the Holy Bible, twelve apostles, each representing one aspect of the soul that needs to be mastered before the soul can be released to higher areas of endeavor.

Thomas Didymus or "Doubting Thomas," as he has come to be known, is a good example of this. The Christ, after his crucifixion at Golgotha, reappeared in his Resurrection body before the apostles. Doubting Thomas, having difficulty in perceiving the truth of "ongoing-life," had to reach out and touch the risen Christ, to make sure within his own mind that this was no dream he was having. To those acquainted with the esoteric nuances of the Bible, there is the recognition that Thomas represented an aspect of our own "Christ-consciousness" that needs to be mastered, i.e., we should not accept things on blind faith, but instead, reach out to find the truth, reach within to our own Christ-consciousness for an acceptance or rejection of that which has been presented. (Cosmic-consciousness is another word for the same meaning.)

To doubt every new idea presented without reaching out to test its validity is much as a negative action, a sign that one has NOT mastered this aspect of his soul. The same holds true of those who receive and accept ideas and dogma with blind faith. The seeking for truth is a positive action, a required action; the acceptance of doctrine or statements without testing them for validity eventually ends in disappointment, heartbreak, and in some cases, with complete loss of religious faith,—a very negative action.

The information presented within this book was given by teachers from higher planes of consciousness than we are presently attuned to; given to us not to glorify them or the channels they work with, but to help mankind to better use and understand one aspect of the mineral kingdom, and to use that information for their own betterment as well as for their fellow-man.

There is much fallow ground for the scientific community to check into if they have mastered the "Thomas-syndrome." Research with galena, mercury, sardonyx and other gem stones might well turn up information that could be of great value to mankind in the decades ahead. As we approach the era of atomic proliferation by many countries, pointing to the prophetic destruction of mankind by fire, wouldn't a little exploration with the use of mercury (as given by the teachers) be prudent in the immediate years ahead? And if this can be proven or developed, would not this be reason to check out other aspects of the mineral kingdom as presented herein? Even with those of less-scientific bent, there will be the questioning of that which has been presented because it is new or not "understandable" to them. We would but ask that you also seek to find the answers.

Almost everyone has a piece of jewelry, a gem, a "worry-stone" or talisman that they have a fondness for. By testing and wearing various stones, see if you can detect any difference between one or the other. Many there are who are extremely sensitive to the auric field of stones and can readily testify to pronounced feelings or emotions when wearing particular gems on their person, while others will experience no inclinations or feelings with any of them. To the latter we can only say that your attunement possibly lies in other areas within your consciousness at the present time. This should not be an indication that the information presented is less valid, or that you are not sub-consciously responding to them. Continue to develop the consciousness of Thomas Didymus and seek out the truth in your own way.

Let us look into another aspect of your "soul-awareness" that needs to be considered by those journeying upon the "higher-path." Many there are who will read this material and recognize and accept the truth within its pages, AND YET, if one of their peers were to question them as to their belief, they would promptly deny that they accept it as truth. ANY time that you are questioned about something that you believe in, and DENY that belief, you are manifesting the negative aspect of the "Peter-syndrome," as it is termed. This aspect of the soul was descriptively portrayed by the apostle "Simon Peter." During the period of the "Last Supper," the Christ turned to Peter and said, "Peter, you will deny me three times ere the cock crows twice." Consider these words, for again, it is a very esoteric statement couched within a traumatic physical drama, but it points out quite clearly a very important aspect of the soul that needs to be mastered. When does a cock crow? At dawn, symbolizing ILLUMINATION, illumination of the "Christ-consciousness" within the soul. This was to say to all who would understand, that you deny the truth within you, your own Christed being, in the physical, the emotional, and in the mental, until one day you become illumined and recognize the Christ is within you just as it was within Jesus. WE ARE ONE! At this juncture in your life, you will begin to stand erect and speak up for what you believe in, be it "life-everlasting," an ideology, or merely a conviction or a belief in a particular thing. When you can take the "plain brown wrapper" off of the book beneath your arm, and KEEP IT OFF, you will know you are well on the way to mastering another aspect of your soul.

There are those who will read this book that have never heard of the seven major chakra centers, the four lower bodies of the soul, the seven Rays or any of the other material of an esoteric nature, but can yet relate quite well to the gem stones on the physical plane. If you fall within this category, we would lay down a challenge to you. Consider the Three Divine Directives within the New Testament of the Holy Bible: 1. Ask, and ye shall receive. 2. Seek, and ye shall find. 3. Knock, and the door shall be opened unto you. Take these within your consciousness and begin to seek the answers, to ask for truth from the best source available to you, be it a person, a book, a study group, a period of meditation, or whatever. The answers will flow as the questions are asked; the door will be opened as the knock is heard, and as ye seek ye will surely find. And when all is said and done, when the ages have passed away, you will then truly know that we ARE all ONE, each a living manifestation and a uniquely expressive facet of God.

May Light and love, peace and understanding be with you each moment of your existence on the journey back home.

Appendix

Tradition has long given us birthstones that would correspond to the month a person was born in. Although the stones
may appear arbitrary, there was still an esoteric reason for
their selection, but this aspect of selection goes into astrology
and corresponding energy patterns, and will not be dealt
with here. They are listed for reference and convenience only.

STONE GROUPINGS BY MONTH
Birth Stones

January	Garnet
February	Amethyst
March	Bloodstone and Aquamarine
April	Diamond
May	Emerald
June	Pearl, Alexandrite and Moonstone
July	Ruby
August	Sardonyx and Peridot
September	Sapphire
October	Opal and Tourmaline
November	Topaz
December	Turquoise and Zircon

Birthstones have also been given a relationship to the Zodiac, and their grouping is listed as follows:

STONE	ZODIACAL CONTROL	PERIOD
Garnet	Aquarius	Jan. 21 to Feb. 21
Amethyst	Pisces	Feb. 21 to Mar. 21
Bloodstone	Aries	Mar. 21 to Apr. 20
Sapphire	Taurus	Apr. 20 to May 21
Agate	Gemini	May 21 to Jun. 21
Emerald	Cancer	Jun. 21 to Jul. 22
Onyx	Leo	Jul. 22 to Aug. 22
Carnelian	Virgo	Aug. 22 to Sep. 22
Peridot	Libra	Sep. 22 to Oct. 23
Aquamarine	Scorpio	Oct. 23 to Nov. 21
Topaz	Sagittarius	Nov. 21 to Dec. 21
Ruby	Capricorn	Dec. 21 to Jan. 21

A closely related idea is found in the 12 stones which, according to the Jewish Cabalists, were supposed to have a mystical power when engraved with certain anagrams. They are as follows:

Ruby-Malchedial	Sapphire-Herchel	Amethyst-Adnachiel
Topaz-Asmodel	Diamond-Humatiel	Beryl-Humiel
Carbuncle-Ambriel	Jacinth-Zuriel	Onyx-Gabriel
Emerald-Muriel	Agate-Barbiel	Jasper-Barchiel

Even the apostolic group were given a correspondence to the stones, and if you can recognize that each of the apostles esoterically symbolized one facet of the soul that needs to be mastered, you will be able to correlate these stones with the astrological zodiac and receive a clue as to which aspect of the soul each apostle was portraying. None was listed for Judas, (the betrayer) but this can be deduced by the process of elimination. For the true seeker, do not doubt the validity of the role Judas portrayed. Each of us betray our own High-self, our own "Christ-consciousness," many times through acts of adultery, falsehoods, deceit, etc., until finally that aspect of our consciousness is mastered or "destroyed," an aspect well portrayed by Judas.

Jasper (bloodstone)	St. Peter
Emerald	St. John
Beryl	St. Thomas
Garnet	St. Simeon
Sapphire	St. Andrew
Sardonyx	St. Philip
Chrysoprase	St. Thaddeus
Amethyst	St. Matthias
Chalcedony	St. James
Carnelian	St. Matthew
Topaz	St. James the Less
?	Judas Iscariot

RELATIONSHIPS BETWEEN STONES, PLANETS AND RAYS

STONE	PLANET	RAY	CRYSTAL CLASS.	RAT-ING
Agate	Earth	Blue-turq.	Trigonal	**
Amethyst	Pluto	Violet	Trigonal	****
Aquamarine	Neptune	Green	Hexagonal	**
Azurite	Neptune	Blue	Monoclinic	*
Beryl	Moon	Milky white	Hexagonal	*
Bloodstone	Mars	Red-orange	Trigonal	***
Carnelian	Saturn's moon	Orange	Trigonal	**
Chalcedony	Moon	Pale blue	Trigonal	***
Chrysoberyl	Venus (reflective)	Pink	Orthorhombic	**

STONE	PLANET	RAY	CRYSTAL CLASS.	RAT- ING
Coral	Neptune	Flat white		*
Crystal (quartz)	Saturn-Neptune	Aquamarine	Trigonal	* * *
Diamond	Neptune	White	Cubic	* * *
Emerald	Moon	Green	Hexagonal	* * * *
Garnet	Mercury	Yellow	Cubic	* * * *
Jade	Jupiter-Pluto	Green	Monoclinic	* * *
Jasper	Mars	Red	Trigonal	*
Kunzite	Pluto	Purple	Monoclinic	*
Lapis Lazuli	Moon	White	Cubic	* * * * *
Malachite	Venus	Dark green	Monoclinic	*
Moonstone	Venus, Neptune, Moon	Pale blue	Monoclinic	*
Onyx	Mars	Red	Trigonal	* * *
Opal	Neptune	Green	Amorphous	*
Pearl	Venus	White	Organic	* *
Peridot	Polaris (North star)	Green	Orthorhombic	* *
Ruby	Noele (new planet)	Red	Trigonal	* *
Sapphire	Venus	Blue	Trigonal	* * *
Sardonyx	Mars	Dark green	Trigonal	* *
Spinel	Pluto & Neptune	Blue-green	Cubic	* *
Tiger's Eye	Saturn	Orange	Trigonal	* * * *
Topaz	Venus (one aspect)	Yellow-green	Orthorhombic	* * *
Tourmaline	Neptune	Pale green	Trigonal	*
Turquoise	Jupiter	Yellow	Triclinic	* * * *
Zircon	Pluto	Emerald green	Tetragonal	*

Note: The use of a "rating" for a stone was an arbitrary one, based upon an evaluation of the information received through "channel." It is recognized each person will place priorities and preferences, based upon their own requirements, likes and dislikes. This was merely put in as a guide for those with no particular preference for stones, but yet might like to acquire and/or wear the gems based upon our evaluations.

One additional grouping evolved as we worked our way through the many varieties of stones, a grouping that will be of particular interest to the esotericist.

CRYSTAL CLASS.	RAY	CHAKRA CENTER
Cubic	Blue	Sacral
Hexagonal	Green	Solar plexus
Tetragonal	Pink	Heart
Orthorhombic	Orange	Will
Monoclinic	Blue-violet	Third Eye
Triclinic	Yellow	Crown
Trigonal	Red	Base

There are many sources for acquiring gem stones. It is recommended that those seeking the "precious" stones should contact gemologists or quality jewelry stores in their locale. Good sources for the semi-precious stones (at reasonable rates) would be through lapidary stores, and through publications, such as "The Lapidary Journal," or "Gems and Minerals."

Bibliography

Esoteric Psychology Book II, Alice A. Baily, Lucis Publishing Co., New York 1970

Esoteric Healing, Alice A. Bailey, Lucis Publishing Co. New York 1970

The Rays and the Initiations, Alice A. Bailey, Lucis Pub. Co., N.Y. 1970

The Secret of Light, Walter Russell, Univ. of Science and Philosophy, Swannanoa, Waynesboro, Va. 22980 1971

Gem Stones, G.F. Herbert Smith, M.A., D.Sc., Methuen & Co. Ltd. 36 Essex Street, W.C. London 1913

Hand Book and Descriptive Catalogue of the Collections of Gems and Precious Stones in the U.S. National Muesum, George P. Merrill, Washington Government Printing Office, 1922

Color Treasury of Crystals, Orbis Publishing Ltd., London, England 1973

Minerals of the World, Charles A. Sorrell, Golden Press, New York

An Introduction to Minerals, J. Ladurner, Pinguin Verlag, Innsbruck, Austria 1968

If you have enjoyed reading this book, you will be interested in another book by the same authors:

THE PATH TO ILLUMINATION
by Wally & Jenny Richardson and Lenora Huett

The material in this book was received in channeling sessions continuing over a four-year period, with Lenora Huett being the channel through which a "higher source" gave teachings and information. Jenny Richardson formulated the questions of a high spiritual nature and those reaching to the soul nature, while Wally coordinated the basic material, supplying many of the basic outline questions.

The guidance of this book can be most helpful to those who are bogged down along life's pathway with questions— questions—questions. Where does one go to seek the truth? Where does truth come from? Why is there so much negativity in the world of today and of yesteryear? This book should bring many answers to each individual soul. At the same time it will most likely take each mind down trails of new questions and seekings. Follow your feelings and your deeper understanding through these pages, let these answers sink into your many levels of consciousness and let the new stream of questions be released. The constantly unfolding path is not only intriguing but as exciting as TOMORROW. —Master of the Mind

"It is our sincere desire that you will use this material as a springboard to greater expansion of your consciousness, in turn doing what you can to help raise the consciousness of all God's children struggling to find the way. The way IS ahead, and the blessings of the Father go with you as you seek."

—The Authors